# Latin America at the End of Politics

# Latin America at the End of Politics

Forrest D. Colburn

**Princeton University Press**

Princeton and Oxford

Copyright © 2002 by Princeton University Press
Published by Princeton University Press, 41 William Street, Princeton, New Jersey 08540
In the United Kingdom: Princeton University Press, 3 Market Place, Woodstock, Oxfordshire OX20 1SY
All Rights Reserved

ISBN 0-691-08907-8 (cl.)
ISBN 0-691-09181-1 (pbk.)

Library of Congress Cataloging-in-Publication Data

Colburn, Forrest D.
    Latin America at the end of politics / Forrest D. Colburn.
    p. cm.
    Includes bibliographical references.
    ISBN 0-691-08907-8 (cloth : alk. paper) — ISBN 0-691-09181-1 (pbk. : alk. paper)
    1. Latin America—Politics and government—1980-   2. Latin America—Economic conditions—1982-   3. Latin America—Social conditions—1982-  I. Title.

JL966 .C65 2002
306'.098—dc21                                 2001038753

British Library Cataloging-in-Publication Data is available

This book has been composed in Sabon

Printed on acid-free paper. ∞

www.pup.princeton.edu

Printed in the United States of America

10 9 8 7 6 5 4 3 2 1

10 9 8 7 6 5 4 3 2 1
(Pbk.)

If the shark is the last one to criticize saltwater,
maybe it does take an outsider to see things.

John Baldessari

---

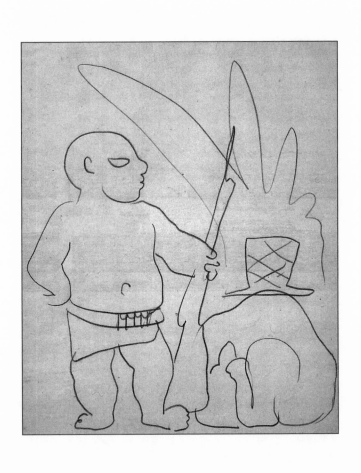

# Contents

# Acknowledgments

This contemplation of Latin America was stimulated by work at INCAE, an institution not well known outside of business and public policy circles in Latin America, though it is perhaps Latin America's premier graduate school of management. (Initially, INCAE was an acronym, but now it is the formal—and only—name of the institute.) INCAE's central campus is in Costa Rica, but half the students in the two-year master's program come from South America. The annual four-week executive program is likewise "continental": participants come from as far as Brazil, Argentina, and Chile as well as Peru, Ecuador, Colombia, and Venezuela, in addition to the countries of Central America and Mexico. Similarly, INCAE's seminars and "in-house" training programs are often held outside of Costa Rica, from Buenos Aires to Quito to Miami. INCAE's faculty not only teach but also do research, principally for the writing of teaching cases and for sponsored projects. Research, too, often takes the faculty far from the tranquil campus in La Garita, Costa Rica. Thus, for INCAE's faculty there is constant travel and constant encounters with a diverse set of Latin Americans. Work is engaging and thought-provoking. In response, and in gratitude, I offer these reflections.

At INCAE I am indebted to many colleagues, including Brizio Biondi-Morra, Roberto Artavia, Ernesto Ayala, Pedro Raventós, Arturo Cruz, Eduardo Montiel, Francisco de Paula Gutiérrez, Alberto Trejos, Tom Bloch, and Danilo Lacayo. I am especially thankful to Ernesto Ayala; late-afternoon conversations with him shaped the design of this work.

My work at INCAE was complemented by teaching stints at Princeton University and the City University of New York (CUNY). At Princeton University I am grateful to Peter Johnson, John Waterbury (who has since moved to Beirut), Robert Socolow, Atul Kohli, James Trussell, Paul Sigmund, Gillett Griffin, and a fellow visiting professor, Jorge Castañeda. At CUNY I was assisted by Xavier Totti, César Ayala, Milagros

Ricourt, Laird Bergad, José Luis Rénique, Herb Broderick, Vinisius Navarro, and Rubén Gallo.

Art to complement the text was graciously provided in New York by Spencer Throckmorton of Throckmorton Fine Art. My wife, Kathrin Colburn, a textile conservator, selected the art in consultation with Spencer. Kathrin also arranged the photography of the art, which was done by her colleagues at the Metropolitan Museum of Art, Bruce Schwarz and Joseph Coscia. A grant from the Shuster Fund paid for the photography.

A colleague at Cornell University, Norman Uphoff, read a first draft of this study during an extended visit to Madagascar, one of the world's poorest countries. He reported finding it quite a juxtaposition to be working and traveling there while considering the travails and paradoxes of a region—Latin America—that has moved far ahead of Madagascar economically, only to confront a whole new set of difficulties. Norman gave me extensive, thoughtful, and inspiring comments that enabled me to strengthen the study.

# Latin America at the End of Politics

# Chapter 1

## Introduction

LATIN AMERICA at the end of politics? Yes, of politics with a capital p. With the electoral defeat of the Sandinistas in Nicaragua, disenchantment with the Cuban Revolution, and arguably even more important, the collapse of socialism in Eastern Europe in 1989 and the dissolution of the Soviet Union in 1991, the impetus in Latin America for remaking state and society has withered. There is an end to ideological confrontation and contestation. What has triumphed, more through default than victory, is liberalism: democracy and capitalism. But it is a particular kind of liberalism. The region's democracies are fragile, inefficient, and chaotic in aggregating and implementing society's preferences. There is considerable politics with a lowercase p. Likewise, there are monopolies, weak regulation, and other impediments to a robust capitalism. However, the more serious shortcoming of the triumphant liberalism— a limitation that defines the era—is that liberalism has been sheared of its close association with egalitarianism. There is, at the end of the twentieth century and the beginning of the twenty-first century, a loss of confidence in the promise of liberalism: to promote equality, at least of opportunity.

What has been lost by the end of "high politics" (or politics with a capital p) is more than faith in the promises of the Bolshevik Revolution. Even the aspirations of the French Revolution, of an inclusive society, of *égalité* and *fraternité*, have been cast aside. The ideal of egalitarianism has been smothered by political fatigue and aspirations for acquisition. It is a period of very modest and carefully circumscribed passions.

The triumph of liberalism has been widely discussed. One of the most cited analyses is Francis Fukuyama's essay "The End of History?" published in the summer 1989 issue of the journal *The National Interest*. The title of the essay is misleading; Fukuyama really discusses the end of politics, not the end of history.

Still, Fukuyama had the prescience to suggest that the prevailing discord in Eastern Europe had a larger significance, that it marked the demise of socialism as an alternative to liberal democracy and to capitalism. Moreover, the demise of socialism was suggested to be of transcendental importance because liberalism now faced no other "challengers," real or imaginable:

> What we may be witnessing is . . . the end point of mankind's ideological evolution and the universalization of Western liberal democracy as the final form of human government.

Surely, as Fukuyama well recognized, there will continue to be noteworthy events, political and otherwise, to attract our attention. Yet, Fukuyama suggests there will be no more fundamental challenges to the central questions of how state and society are organized.

This outcome is a surprise:

> The twentieth century saw the developed world descend into a paroxysm of ideological violence, as liberalism contended first with the remnants of absolutism, then bolshevism and fascism, and finally an updated Marxism that threatened to lead to the ultimate apocalypse of nuclear war. But the century that began full of self-confidence in the ultimate triumph of Western liberal democracy seems at its close to be returning full circle to where it started: not to an "end of ideology" or a convergence between capitalism and socialism, as earlier predicted, but to an unabashed victory of economic and political liberalism.

The poorer parts of the world—Asia, the Middle East, Africa, and Latin America—were likewise damaged by the ideological turmoil of the century, at times because of competition among local groups with contending visions of how to govern, and at other times because poor countries became pawns in the struggles among the wealthy and powerful countries of the world.

In comparison with the rest of the world, Latin America was perhaps least affected by the ideological debates of the twentieth century. The region was not torn apart by fascist movements—or fascist invaders—or the victim of governments hell-bent on a "great leap forward" to "scientific communism." But ideologies, all of them fashioned in Europe, did have a significant impact on Latin America in the twentieth century. They offered political elites visions of state and society, and they shaped public policy. And, so, the "end of politics"—the end of struggle among competing ideologies—is consequential for Latin America.

Latin America begins the twenty-first century with a near-universal embrace of liberal democracy. It is timely to inquire how well the institutions of democracy are working, how well they are fulfilling their responsibilities, in this particular corner of the world. But an inquiry should be broad. The issue is not just how well liberal democracy suits the region, but how it works without the strong voice of proponents of socialism, who were long a vocal presence in Latin America. Ultranationalists, though never quite so numerous, have also been marginalized. In other words, how does democracy work without the constant specter of alternative contenders? Indeed, since what has happened is that alternative ideologies have been discredited, and not that liberalism has been vigorously embraced on its own merits, it is perhaps fairer to ask how democratic institutions—and capitalism—work without serious ideological competition.

It is seductive to think that, at least in the case of Latin America, the functioning of democratic institutions and practices is facilitated by ideological consensus or even by ideological somnolence. But that conclusion would be facile. Democracy depends on choices, among contending candidates and among alternative programs of government. And democracy depends on opposition—on a loyal opposition to be sure, but on a vigorous opposition nonetheless. Underlying everything is the need for public participation. Perhaps ideological heterogeneity—in the case of poor countries—is needed to stimulate political choice, invigorate public participation, and prevent collusion among the political elite.

Throughout the twentieth century, Latin America was galvanized by numerous and almost sequential efforts at redistributing wealth and income. Each effort may have been centered in a particular country, but all had wide repercussions, goading elites elsewhere to pay at least some attention to issues of social equality. The most notable of these bids included the Mexican Revolution and the ensuing reforms of Lázaro Cárdenas, the regime of Getúlio Vargas in Brazil, "Peronism" in Argentina, the Bolivian Revolution in 1952, the Cuban Revolution, the 1968 coup d'état by reformist military officers in Peru, the administration of Salvador Allende in Chile, and the Nicaraguan Revolution. During this extended period, even governments that embraced "free markets" did so cautiously, with some apologies, out of fear that too total a commitment to markets would be perceived as mean. Arguably, the strength of the "left" as a political force—or at least as a threat—compelled Latin American states to be as humane—or as benign—as they were in the past century. What will now elicit compassion from state and society in Latin America?

Thus, there are important questions to ask about Latin America at the end of the twentieth century—and the beginning of the twenty-first century. Yes, it appears that we have come to an end point of ideological evolution, and that the universalization of liberal democracy and the unfettered markets of capitalism are the final forms of government and economic organization. But how well do these servants function in Latin America? Do they suit the idiosyncrasies of the region? And do they work the better for the absence of ideological competition? What sort of society are they spawning? These are pertinent questions without obvious answers.

There is another compelling issue, related but still distinct. As Fukuyama adroitly acknowledges, the end of politics—or as he says, "history"—has wide implications. Politics has more than an ephemeral relationship not just to economic organization and social structure, but also to culture. Just as the withering of socialism in Eastern Europe and the Soviet Union—and in China, too—has undermined faith in socialism, so the triumph of liberalism has amplified the sirens of the largest and most successful case of liberalism: the United States. What

Fukuyama labels the "consumerist Western culture" has spread, and very prominently in Latin America. Advances in technology (especially in transportation and the sharing of information) and expanding trade have helped disseminate the social habits and cultural tastes of the United States and other successful liberal regimes. Here, too, useful inquiries can be made to measure the extent to which the triumph of liberalism in Latin America has been accompanied by changes in local culture, in particular from a desire to imitate the United States.

The urgency for questioning the impact of the "end of politics" on culture comes from the long association in Latin America between the "left" and nationalism, and between the "left" and an insistence on an autochthonous culture. Others who argued vigorously for an autochthonous culture were, perhaps paradoxically, those at the other end of the political spectrum, those on the far "right." What are the cultural implications of "pruning" the ideological spectrum?

This contemplation of Latin America accepts Fukuyama's premise that the exhaustion of viable systematic alternatives to liberalism—to democracy and to capitalism—is a profound event. I do not assume that the change is good, and I do not assume it is pernicious. And I do not assume, either, that the change will last forever. But—for the moment—the collapse of all utopian ideologies marks the end of an era, and provides a starting point for a broad inquiry of Latin America at the end of one century and the beginning of another. Here I attempt to answer in an inductive way two central questions: (1) How does liberalism, which has been interpreted in Latin America as presidential democracy and unfettered markets, both shorn of any meaningful commitment to equality, "fit" the region? (2) What social and cultural changes have followed—or at least accompanied—the celebrated ascension of democracy and capitalism?

These two questions are addressed with a collage: a set of discrete essays, each exploring a different dimension of contemporary Latin America. The intent is to juxtapose descriptive detail with abstraction in a way that engages and illuminates the complexities of the region. Throughout this collage individual experiences abound, and so do arcane—but telling—facts and figures. Interspersed are generalizations and propositions.

The essays appear as chapters, but their sequence is inconsequential; they could easily have been shuffled. Moreover, other topics could have been explored, also used as windows to peer into Latin America at the passing of one century and the start of another. There are an endless variety of wonders and experiences in Latin America, and no effort to be comprehensive could be successful. I was only selective.

The task before me is not to respond to narrow questions, amenable to answer through the identification and marshaling of a particular kind of evidence. Instead, the questions I pose are sweeping: how to fathom an enormous region at a moment of time, an unsettling period when previous paradigms for understanding have lost their grip. These grand questions can be answered for now only with ideas and images. Still, good ideas and images are useful. Indeed, there are times when ideas and images contribute to more understanding than the simple compilation of knowledge.

In addition to contributing, in a general but nuanced way, to our understanding of Latin America, the approach taken—that of moving frequently between individual experiences and generalizations—aspires to generate *empathy*. I remember discussing with a distinguished Princeton scholar, Robert Tucker, an article on politics we had both just read in an academic journal. I mentioned that I found it unsatisfactory. "Yes," he said, "there are no people in it." It was a simple but devastating comment. The best "theorizing" is said to be abstract and parsimonious. But here I stray, preferring to go back to particular individuals, to suggestive places, not just to explore nuances, but also to generate empathy for Latin Americans and the difficult choices they confront.

I also seek to contribute to the rehabilitation of the study of geographical regions, understood to be demarcated not only by their physical geography, but also by shared history, culture, and politics. Studying regions, and even individual nation-states, has fallen out of academic favor. There is a marked pointillism in recent scholarship, with ever more ingenious trawling of archives or statistical databases, either for information on subaltern communities and their struggles, or for insights into the behavior of small groups pursuing their interests in a well-defined arena. The attempt to see the larger picture through new eyes is rarely risked. Yet the nation-state, as vast and lumbering as it may be, remains the locus of most important political decisions. And the behavior of individual nation-states is often heavily influenced by the tack of neighboring states with which there is an affinity. This study is a return to the tradition of asking big questions about nation-states and clusters of nation-states. If its arguments—or even its approach—manage to encourage others into thinking, too, about the larger picture, it will have served one of its main purposes.

It would be fallacious to suggest that this study is entirely inductive. My search through the clutter of Latin America is guided, if only faintly, by a murky collection of hunches, beliefs, worries, and passions. Despite occasional pretensions to the contrary, every work of scholarship is noetic and, upon completion, an incarnation: the envelopment of a subject with a *mentalité* or a set of ideas. So, in a sense, all scholarship is an "assemblage."

Detailing just what set of concerns has guided me is difficult. I have concluded, though, that there is a salient dilemma in Latin America. The end of ideological contestation has lessened political conflict in the region, but it has also lessened the sense of urgency for solving trenchant problems of poverty and social inequality. I worry that there is now an acceptance of inequality with only minimal efforts at remediation or palliation. And I sense that the persistence of stark class divisions reinforces—or heightens—the rugged individualism of liberalism. The lack of *égalité* and *fraternité* complicates the performance of liberalism, of representative democracy and of capitalism, and, moreover, breeds social tension and cultural ambivalence.

Another worry is that liberalism in Latin America is, at least presently, unprepared to offer public solutions to serious collective problems, for example, of urban bias, crime, and environmental degradation. Instead, there are—at least to date—only piecemeal individual strategies for coping with these and other problems. States in Latin America are weak, and in this era of celebrating individual rights there are not determined efforts by political actors to strengthen state capacity. Yet, successful liberal regimes, including prominently the United States, have employed the state—sometimes extensively—to ensure domestic stability and to guide international economic adjustment. Efforts to build stable and prosperous societies in Latin America under the guidance of liberalism are hobbled not only by poverty and inequality, but also frequently by the inability to complement individual initiatives with effective public policies.

Another conviction is that the outcomes of Latin America's wholesale adoption of liberalism at the end of the twentieth century are shaped in many subtle ways by the region's own particular history and constitution. In so many discussions there appears to be the unstated assumption that if other regions of the world embrace the liberalism born and nurtured in Western Europe and North America, they are going to look—politically, economically, and maybe even culturally—like Western Europe and North America, perhaps a comforting thought for some. This assumption is naïve. Liberalism may be the paradigm of the era, even appearing to be the "peak of ideological evolution," but nation-states embracing liberalism may well be—and remain—very different from one another. Liberalism is compatible with many different outcomes.

Assuaging these concerns, I acknowledge that democracy and capitalism have the virtues of being dynamic—ever in flux—and also malleable. Shortcomings and undesired outcomes can be addressed within the paradigm—or ideological construct—of liberalism. And in any case, nothing in politics is ever really final. So what I can offer here is not a definitive evaluation of liberalism in Latin America. I can only hope to illuminate Latin America at a particular point in time, a moment when, incongruously as it may seem in the future, it truly appears to be "at the end of politics."

# Chapter 2

## Latin America as a Place

Lᴀᴛɪɴ Aᴍᴇʀɪᴄᴀ is the proper noun used to describe the geographical region and encompassing nation-states of Mexico, Central America, the islands of the Caribbean, and South America. The term is inconsistently used. Mexico is geographically part of North America. Latin America sometimes refers not just to numerous Spanish-speaking countries, Portuguese-speaking Brazil, French-speaking Haiti, and the French West Indies, but also countries such as Suriname, Guyana, and the many English-speaking island states of the Caribbean where Romance languages are not spoken. At other times Latin America refers exclusively to Spanish- and Portuguese-speaking countries, including, thus, only Cuba, the Dominican Republic, and Puerto Rico in the Caribbean. Belize is not included, being relegated to the Caribbean, as are Suriname, Guyana, and French Guiana. The non–Spanish-speaking nations—or territories—of the Caribbean are often held to differ not just in language, but culturally and politically, too. At still other times Haiti is included in the universe of Latin America, seemingly because it has been an independent nation since 1804, and perhaps, too, because it shares the island of Hispaniola with the Dominican Republic. There is considerable confusion.

The term Latin America did not exist in the lexicon until well past the period when most of the countries of the region became independent nations. The first names for the region were Nuevo Mundo, América, América del Sur, and América Meridional. The considerable portion that was under Spanish colonial rule was also called América Española and Hispanoamérica. The term Latin America originated in France during the reign of Napoleon III in the 1860s, when the country was second only to England in terms of industrial and financial strength. The French intellectual Michel Chevalier, in an effort to solidify the political underpinnings of French colonial ambitions, proposed a "Pan-Latin" foreign policy in the hopes of promoting solidarity among nations whose languages were of Latin origin and whose populations shared the common cultural tradition of Roman Catholicism. Led by France, the reasoning went, Latin peoples could reassert their influence throughout the world in the face of threats from both the Slavic peoples of eastern Europe (led by Russia) and the Anglo-Saxon peoples of northern Europe (led by England). In the Western Hemisphere, intellectuals seized upon the term l'Amérique latine to distinguish between the "Anglo" north and the "Latin" south. Thus, from the French l'Amérique latine, the term—and conception of a unified region—came into use in other languages, including Spanish, Portuguese, and English.

The term Latin America has been criticized not only for its imprecision, but also for advancing representations of an assumed cultural homogeneity that contributes to legitimating social discrimination. During the colonial period, it is argued, European and mestizo elites began building new nation-states upon a prevalent system of exclusions. These elites assumed that they, not the so-called *indios*, or the imported African slaves and their descendants, were "the people."

The interdependent creation of both national identities and an all-encompassing, pannational "Latin American" identity has not ceased. There persist efforts to suggest that a language (or a pair of related Romance languages) and a colonial and postcolonial history are the common and distinctive features shared by the millions of inhabitants of the region (*latinoamericanos*), as if it was a sort of undifferentiated extended family. As Daniel Mato argues in the spring/fall 1997 issue of *The Latino Review of Books*:

> Such a pretension has its own mythology of origin which has been long crafted through educational systems and other social institutions, beginning with the arrival of Columbus and the subsequent process of *mestizaje*. The European roots have been overemphasized everywhere, while the American and African roots—and to a lesser extent others—have been practically ignored in . . . Latin American states. This "mestizo" identity has been crucial in providing meaning and legitimization to diverse social, cultural, and economic mechanisms that have historically undermined the situation of both indigenous peoples and the diverse populations constituted by the descendants of African slaves.

What is at stake is more, too, than opportunities for cultural autonomy and expression. There is a strong relationship between race and class in Latin America. And Latin America is the most inequitable region in the world (with no "floor"); being at the bottom of the rigid class structure relegates one to poverty.

The nations of Latin America, though, have accomplished the basic tasks of nation-building, even if in a clumsy and inequitable manner. The nations of the region are *governed*. The central institutions of government are in place; anarchy is rare, as is communal violence. Moreover, the region has not suffered—at least in the twentieth century—from inter-state warfare. There is considerable economic development; the World Bank describes the region as "middle income."

The decisive political unit in Latin America is the nation-state; that is where consequential decisions are made. Nothing of any importance is decided at the regional level, indeed, there is no political unit representing the region of Latin America. (The Organization of American States includes the United States and Canada [Fidel Castro dismisses it as the colonial office of Washington], and—in any case—it is feeble.) Likewise, individuals' political identification is not first and foremost with the region, but instead with their particular nation. The nation-states of Latin America vary in size, constitution, and political history, reflecting the vagaries of geography, colonial settlement, indigenous population, immigration, elite divisions, class conflict, the skill of successive governors, and interaction with other countries, especially the United States and the countries of Western Europe. Still, there are linkages among the countries of the region. The locus of decision-making may be the state, but at times there are powerful "currents" that lead political actors in different nations to make similar decisions within a relatively compressed period of time.

One such instance was in the 1980s, a decade of sweeping and transcendental changes in Latin America. At the beginning of the decade the majority of countries in the region were governed by authoritarian—military—regimes that pursued statist economic policies. But by the first few years of the following decade, the 1990s, all of the countries except Cuba had constitutional governments, elected in free and competitive elections. The case of Mexico needs to be qualified; the ruling party had yet to lose a presidential election (since its founding in 1929), but at least the symbols and rituals of democracy were evident, and the party's elite promised to move the country to a genuine competitive democracy. (And they, in fact, did surrender power in the aftermath of their defeat in the 2000 elections.) Even with this qualification, Latin America's abrupt embrace of liberal democracy in the 1980s was remarkable.

Moreover, there was a second major shift in the 1980s—the adoption of market-based economic policies. And here there were no exceptions. Even Cuba, under the continued leadership of a Communist party (or at least of a leader—Fidel Castro—who pledged continued allegiance to communism), altered economic policy to give freer rein to markets. (As a historian at the University of Havana told me, this unlikely combination has resulted in considerable "*confusión*.")

Never before in the history of Latin America have so many countries—nearly all—been so thoroughly committed to government by the tenets of liberalism and to management of the economy, too, by the tenets of liberalism. The era is without precedent. Early in the twentieth century, many Latin American governments favored open economies, but rulers were imposed by either oligarchies or the military. At the middle of the century, many Latin American governments were democratically elected, but they pursued statist economic policies that sought to constrain markets. The combination of the 1990s—a period of democracy and free markets—is novel. Just as important, this change of paradigms is all but uncontested. There are no perceived alternatives, which seemingly fortifies liberal doctrine and practice. A century of ideological contestation, which was fanned by the Cuban Revolution in 1959, came to a quiet close.

Liberalism and democracy are often conflated, including prominently in Latin America. Liberalism is best understood as constitutional and limited government, the rule of law, and the protection of individual rights. Democracy, in contrast, is understood as the selection of governors by universal suffrage in free, competitive elections. Conceivably, there are regimes that can plausibly be called democratic but not liberal. It is probably easier to hold genuinely free elections than to fulfill liberalism's commitment to the rule of law. The initial priority in Latin America's movement away from authoritarianism certainly was the holding of elections. But Latin American countries have attempted to be "liberal democracies," fulfilling the aspirations of both liberalism (for rule by law and for respect of human rights) and democracy (with its insistence on the election of rulers). As elsewhere, liberal ideals and democratic procedures have become interwoven.

The liberalism of the late eighteenth and the nineteenth centuries, though, was also committed to equality. The American Declaration of Independence proclaims as the first of its self-evident truths "that all men are created equal." The French Declaration of the Rights of Man and Citizen states: "Men are born, and always continue, free and equal in respect of their rights." The relationship between the rights or freedom of men—and women—and their equality can be traced back to the opening pages of the classic work of liberal political theory, John Locke's *Second Treatise of Government*. In describing the natural state of "man," he says this is not only "a state of perfect freedom," but also "a state of equality, wherein all the power and jurisdiction is reciprocal, no one having more than another." In the liberal states of the North Atlantic—the United Kingdom, France, the United States, and Canada—the relationship between freedom (especially to acquire and own property) and equality has been vexed. But equality—at least of opportunity—has been viewed as desirable, and there has been a concurrent concern for how inequality undermines democracy. Consequently, the machinery of government has been used in a myriad of ways to promote equality. There have also always existed private initiatives.

Although it is difficult to generalize for all of Latin America, it seems that throughout the region a concomitant concern for equality is missing. Absent is a sense of how liberalism—with its foundation of commitment to individual rights—has historically been tied to an appreciation for equality. It is as if the drive in country after country was just to oust authoritarian rulers, imposed upon the nation, who had run roughshod over laws and human rights. Competitive elections, rule by law, and respect for human rights would provide sufficient relief. Why stop there? Perhaps the mention of equality evoked unpleasant memories of the conflict associated with previous efforts at redistributing wealth and income. Or, perhaps, powerful—and moneyed—elites were happy to jettison inept authoritarian leaders, and live with the uncertainty of democracy, as long as redistributive issues were kept off the table. It is not clear why the shearing of equality occurred. But today, in sum, Latin America has embraced not just democracy, but liberal democracy—minus its historical concern for equality.

The concurrent embrace of economic liberalism led to many reforms that had as their first priority pulling countries out of the region's worst depression since the 1930s. However, these reforms invariably strengthened markets and the role of entrepreneurship. These reforms included fiscal overhaul (with the purpose of slashing inflation-generating deficits), interest- and exchange-rate adjustment, tax reform, trade liberalization, deregulation, and privatization. Welfare benefits—including, for example, food subsidies—have commonly been cut, in part to reduce government expenditures and in part to end market distortions (which might stifle entrepreneurs).

These reforms have differed in kind and pace from country to country in Latin America. In many countries the state, while weakened, remains a powerful economic actor. Everywhere, however, there has been considerable change; there is more reliance on markets, and so there is more competition. Protective tariffs, for example, have plummeted. Between 1985 and 1992, the average tariff fell from 80 percent to 21 percent in Brazil, from 34 percent to 4 percent in Mexico, from 28 percent to 15 percent in Argentina, from 83 percent to 7 percent in Colombia, and from 30 percent to 17 percent in Venezuela, to take five of the largest economies. Even in the small, poor counties of Central America, though, protective tariffs have fallen, from an average of 63 percent in the 1980s to an average of 11 percent by the end of the 1990s. Also noteworthy, the inflation rate in Latin America—as a region—declined from 1,200 percent in 1989 to 10 percent in 1997. This decline in protective tariffs and in inflation has stimulated a boom in international trade, and trade, in turn, stimulates competition among firms.

Reflecting the political tone of the era, there is less commitment to equality. The government enters the economy to help markets to be efficient, not to direct them to better meet the needs of the poor and disenfranchised. The president of one of Latin America's central banks told me, in a frank but discreet conversation, that the position of his government is, "it is only going to do what is necessary to provide macro economic stability; what happens after that is up to the private sector." This stance is common.

Throughout Latin America the economic reforms of the era are frequently called "neoliberal." But the prefix "neo" is added only to distinguish them from some never-defined earlier set of economic policies.

With its emphasis on individual economic rights, and competition among individuals and firms in markets, Latin America's reigning economic paradigm is naked liberalism, untempered by social concerns. Liberalism in economic matters, though, is seemingly more open to interpretation than liberalism in governance. Even in poor countries, the economies of today are complex. There are many details—many technical questions—for which an economic philosophy alone is inadequate as a guide for decision-making. Liberalism can afford many differences in public policies.

How did so many countries in Latin America, each unique, come to embrace liberalism at the end of the twentieth century? This is a puzzle. The depression of the 1980s certainly put enormous pressure on existing regimes, most of them authoritarian. It also discredited statist management of the economy. The rising misfortunes of socialism in Eastern Europe and elsewhere discredited the ideology, and so undermined regimes whose *raison d'être* was defending the country against *comunismo*. The democratic opening in Spain upon the death of General Francisco Franco in 1975 was closely followed in Latin America; President Felipe González adroitly pursued market-oriented economic policies as he helped consolidate Spain's incipient democracy. The economic success of such East Asian countries as South Korea was also suggestive. But enumerating all of the variables, and assigning them explanatory weight, is a daunting task.

Each country must be studied individually to trace specific outcomes. Even to erstwhile authoritarian leaders, liberalism may have seemed inevitable, but the *timing* and the *terms* of the transition needed to be negotiated by local political actors. Still, the synchronic sweep of the changes suggest that while the decisions to embrace liberalism were made in each country, there were powerful international "currents" that induced and pushed these decisions throughout the region within a brief span of time, really little more than a decade.

Some have attempted to describe and explain the transition from authoritarianism to democracy in Latin America. Others have measured the impact of entrusting the economy to markets. Still others have explored the relationship between political change and economic reform. Me, I wonder where these changes, all so unforeseen, are taking us.

.

# Chapter 3

## Urban Bias

THE GREATEST difference between human life in 1900 and 2000 is simply that there is more of it, well over three times more, a rate of population growth unlike any that preceded it. Latin American countries have had some of the world's highest population growth rates, well above the average. For example, in 1900 Mexico's population was 13.6 million. In 1940 its population was 19.6 million. In 1970 its population was 48.2 million. In 1990 its population was 81.2 million. Sometime around 2000 Mexico's population will pass 100 million, representing more than a sevenfold increase in one century.

Another pronounced demographic trend is urbanization. Advances in agriculture have permitted human settlement to move from being primarily rural to being primarily urban in less than a hundred years. In 1900 only Great Britain had less than half of its population working the land. At the beginning of the twentieth century roughly 90 percent of the world's population lived outside cities, mainly on farms. Now less than half of the world's population lives in rural settings. Cities have grown exponentially in population since 1900, particularly in the poorer countries of the world. For example, returning to Mexico, its rural population doubled in the twentieth century; its urban population increased fifteenfold during the same period. Urbanization is a powerful trend, with many complex but poorly understood consequences.

All of Latin America has undergone rapid urbanization, a trend that continues apace. Indeed, it is expected that early in the twenty-first century Latin America will be the most urbanized region in the world. The sway of cities—and capitals in particular—over countries throughout Latin America is notable. Indeed, there are countries in the region where the name of the capital is the same as the nation-state itself: México and México, Guatemala and Guatemala, San Salvador and El Salvador, and Panamá and Panamá. And throughout Latin America, capital cities are commonly home to between a fifth and a third of the national population. Populations are concentrated in capital cities even in countries that are large and when the region as a whole has only a fifth the population density of Asia. The most pronounced case is Argentina, a country nearly the size of India (which has a population of one billion). Roughly a third of Argentina's 36 million inhabitants live in the greater Buenos Aires metropolitan region.

Urbanization is in part a seemingly inevitable outcome of economic development. Yet urbanization, in Latin America at least, is also a political outcome. The Mexican poet Octavio Paz once remarked that there is an organic relationship between power and cities. Capitals are the center of political power; government budgets invariably are disproportionately dispersed in the capital, sometimes grossly so. Other political prerogatives are also concentrated in the capital, and are more accessible to those residing in the capital. Even political protest is more effective in the capital. Peasants clamoring in the countryside can be ignored; protest in front of the national palace is a threat.

No one has more succinctly described the sway of cities in the less-developed countries of the world than Michael Lipton with his phrase "urban bias." He persuasively argues that small, interlocking urban elites substantially control the distribution of resources. The power of the urban elite is tied to their leverage over economic resources and government but, more broadly, also to their capacity to organize, control, communicate, and engage in transactions. Rural people are much more dispersed, poor, inarticulate, and unorganized. Consequently, the prosaic working of personal and group self-interest in less-developing countries has led to wide disparities between urban and rural standards of living. There is an expression in Venezuela's capital that is all-telling: "Caracas is Caracas; everything else is snakes and jungle." The arrogance—or urban bias—behind this quip is common throughout Latin America. Indeed, in Haiti those who lives outside of Port-au-Prince are called *moun andeyò*, literally, "outside people," outsiders.

The rural poor of Latin America have instinctively grasped their subordinate status and have flocked to cities, in particular their respective capitals. Rural migration, combined with high rates of population growth, has led to an explosive growth of the capital cities of Latin America. Two of the five largest agglomerations in the world are in Latin America: São Paulo and Mexico City. There are three other enormous metropolitan regions in Latin America: Buenos Aires, Rio de Janeiro, and Lima. But it is not the sheer size of cities in Latin America that is noteworthy—or problematic. What is worrisome is how the rapid growth of cities has led to an atomization of society: an absence of community, a lack of infrastructure (public goods), an inability of governors to offer needed social services, an ugly side-by-side contrast of munificence and poverty, a concentration of pollution, and an impoverished rural sector that is increasingly neglected.

Latin America's cities—and the region's capitals in particular—increasingly pose an uncomfortable paradox. These sprawling cities are political, decision-making, financial, corporate, media, and cultural centers. Indeed, they are often more than centers of these important activities; they sometimes exercise a virtual monopoly. So for many, above all the well educated and ambitious, there is no recourse but to live in the capital. Yet at the same time growth—and the haphazard nature of the growth—has made living in the prominent cities unbearable. The cities are overpopulated (in relation to their infrastructure), unmanageable, and even insalubrious. Thus, for example, it is not surprising that polls suggest that 60 percent of the residents of São Paulo—*Paulistanos*—would like to leave the city.

The unhealthy status and troubled condition of Latin America's great urban centers—its cities—suggests a questioning of reigning attitudes toward politics and economics. The region's governments, with little more than a laissez-faire attitude toward economic development, have not encountered solutions to the urban bias so prominent in Latin America, or to its consequences of unmanageable cities and neglected rural areas. The problems of urban Latin America seemingly require greater attention to public welfare and the political resources to ensure that collective needs are met.

The region's governments—a set of fragile democracies (with a few rough edges here and there)—seem unable to offer more than meek efforts to revamp individual incentives through such policy instruments as taxes (or tax exemptions), assorted restrictions, and subsidies. There can also be public investments, but at least in Latin America these are inevitably meager. These limited political resources are no match for the powerful individual incentives to move to the city or, once there, to stay there. Liberalism's first calling is to protect individual rights, even when evidence accumulates that the rational pursuit of self-interest leads to hellish traffic jams, deadly concentrations of pollution, and other undesirable outcomes of unchecked urbanization.

Mexico City, which by some accounts is now the largest metropolitan region in the world, illustrates just how unmanageable urbanization can be in Latin America. There are different ways of measuring the size of Mexico City: the city proper or the "greater metropolitan area." Using the latter definition, it is estimated that in 1950 the population was 3 million. In 1970 the population of the city was 12 million. The estimate for 2000 is 22 million. But data are not reliable. Supposedly, when the German writer Günter Grass visited the city—years back—he asked what its population was. The range between the answers he was given was 3 million, the size of his native Berlin at the time. But at 22 million, give or take a few million, Mexico City is the largest city in the world. It is home to 22 percent of all Mexicans, even when the territory of the country is enormous—Mexico is the fourteenth largest country in the world.

As enormous as Mexico City is, the territory it covers cannot represent more than one percent of Mexico's national territory—it is, as has been said, "a drop in the sea." Nonetheless, Mexico City generates 37 percent of Mexico's economic output, its gross national product (GNP).

It is estimated that there are forty thousand industrial plants in Mexico City, producing 50 percent of the country's industrial output. Some of these "industrial plants" produce nothing more complicated than tortillas, but within the dense city are factories producing such things as cement, soap and detergents, chemicals, building materials (even asbestos), paper, asphalt, pesticides, pharmaceuticals, metal products, and glass. Industry produces 40 percent of Mexico City's noxious air pollution, including its most toxic components.

Most of the remaining 60 percent of Mexico City's air pollution is produced by vehicles: cars, buses, and trucks. Of late, car ownership has increased rapidly, faster than the rate of the city's population growth. Traffic is more than congested.

Meeting the needs of such an enormous—and ever-growing—city is a daunting task for governors. And it is not clear that they have the necessary authority to solve problems. For example, the quality of air in Mexico City is horrible, so bad that it is a threat to public health. The emissions of such a large, concentrated population are made even more threatening by the city's topography. Mountains and volcanic peaks enclose the city, with air entering or leaving the high-altitude basin only in the southwest of the city. Mexico City experiences exceptional ozone levels. Another danger is "suspended particulates," windblown dust and toxic "particles" from—among other sources—open-air garbage dumps and dried sewage disposal sites. Breathing the air of Mexico City is said to be the equivalent of inhaling pollutants from forty cigarettes a day. It is claimed that a significant percentage of the city's residents suffer from diseases caused or aggravated by air pollution.

What has the government done—what is it doing—about air pollution? The government has not questioned the "right" to generate pollution; it has instead sought to moderate sources of pollution. For example, in 1989 the government began the "No Circulation Today" scheme: all private vehicles registered in the city must display one of five color-coded permits in which each color represents a weekday in which the vehicle is not to be used. (The wealthy—and so politically powerful—circumvent this measure by having more than one vehicle.) During "smog alerts," reductions in industrial emissions are set, the use of government vehicles is reduced, and street repairs are halted to minimize traffic jams. Trees have been planted in the surrounding mountains. Since efforts to moderate Mexico City's air pollution began in the late 1980s, no significant improvement has been noted, in part because the continuing growth of the city simply offsets or outweighs any gains from (politically inoffensive but feeble) government polices to reduce pollution. As a former mayor of Mexico City once remarked, "Attending to Mexico City's problems is like trying to service a jet while it is in flight."

Another serious problem in Mexico City—and one that overwhelms governors—is the provision of water. There are said to be twenty-one public agencies involved in the supply of water to Mexico

City. Despite their efforts, the extraction of water from the Valley of Mexico—once a valley of lakes—far exceeds its replacement. Water tables are falling dramatically. Moreover, the high rates of extraction of water have degraded the quality of remaining water and created the risk of the water table being contaminated with wastewater. Finally, the draining of water from underground reservoirs has led to the sinking of Mexico City, by an average of ten centimeters a year but in certain areas up to forty centimeters a year. This sinking not only causes damage to buildings, but also further disrupts the water system.

Despite these and other problems, Mexico City remains the center of Mexico. Per capita incomes in Mexico City are higher than elsewhere in the country. Also, opportunities for education—including for the poor—are greater, too, in Mexico City than elsewhere. But residents of Mexico City are acutely aware of the city's problems—and the extent to which these problems compromise their welfare—and of the government's inability to provide redress. Many feel trapped. At best they can, if their means allow for it, seek individual solutions to what are collective problems. Homes and offices have air filters, water filters, water tanks (to cope with shortages), private guards, and other "necessities." Those less fortunate get along as best they can, grateful for a relative gain over their rural brethren.

The obverse of the prominence of Mexico City in Mexico, and prominence, too, of other cities throughout the country, is large swaths of rural areas that are marginalized. It is estimated that 10 million Mexicans are subsistence farmers—peasants—eking out a precarious livelihood from the land. Peasants are most concentrated in poor—and rural—states like Michoacán, Guerrero, Oaxaca, and Chiapas. As in centuries past, the most important determinant of their welfare is the season's rains. Their Mexico may be picturesque, *folklórico*, with *sombreros, tortillas, burros*, and *nopales*. But their poverty—their backwardness—is not endearing.

Earlier in the twentieth century there were at least intermittent efforts to ameliorate rural poverty through agrarian reform and an eclectic array of policies and projects lumped together under the rubric of "rural development." But in Mexico—as elsewhere in Latin America—this kind of state intervention has fallen out of favor. No one talks anymore about agrarian reform; there are no more subsidies for fertilizer; agricultural extension agents have vanished. If peasants are dissatisfied, they, as a "factor of production," have the freedom, the liberty, to move to where they can be "more productively employed."

I was driving with a friend through the mountains of Guerrero, driving on unpaved roads that link desolate villages. Between two villages we encountered an older man walking. I suggested we offer him a ride. Feigning ignorance, I asked him a number of questions. He knew the state capital was Chilpancingo. He knew Mexico City was the capital of the country, the seat of the government, but he had never been there. No, he did not vote. And, no, he did not know the name of the current president of Mexico. But, he added, he did know that the president was not Mexican. "Oh, where is he from?" "He is Spanish," was the enigmatic reply.

*El distrito está muy federal* is a collection of the work of twenty cartoonists who present their commentary on Mexico City. In one cartoon a stork is sprawled on the ground, stars dancing above its head. Beside it is a bawling baby. The stork could not enter Mexico City to make its delivery. The outline of the city's borders is shown, with the city packed with screaming people, climbing over one another. There is no room. In another cartoon there is a profile portrait of a man with a bloodshot eye. A car is stuck in his mouth, and smoke pours out of his ear. Another cartoon shows a robber "lifting" the wallet of some helpless person. Behind the robber is an angel with a raised club. But behind the angel is the devil with an even larger, raised club. Another cartoon shows two peasants standing next to a miserable shack, all at the top of a mountain. The peasants peer down into the Valley of Mexico, where Mexico City is just a blur of black smoke. Looking into the mess, the peasants comment, "poor people."

A Mexican intellectual, Gonzalo Celorio, has said that the history of Mexico City is a story of successive periods of destruction and rebirth. The remaking of the city has followed sweeping political change: the conquest, colonialism, independence, and—now a long time ago—the Mexican Revolution. Notwithstanding its cultural richness, Mexico City now seems "apocalyptic"—as some say in Mexico, a time bomb. What will bring relief, rebirth? Will new technology, as yet unimagined, bring relief from congestion and environmental degradation? Or will only traumatic political change—even more unimaginable—be necessary to halt urban bias, and the dominance of Mexico City in particular? Or will nothing change, including the city's continued growth? What happens to Mexico City will be followed with keen interest elsewhere in Latin America: too many of the region's cities are following the reckless path of Mexico City.

# Chapter 4

## An Ideological Vacuum

JOSÉ FIGUEROA does not understand why the Plaza de España supermarket in Managua sells frozen Minute Maid orange juice imported from the United States when a dozen poor Nicaraguans hawk bags of sweet oranges in the supermarket's parking lot. He is bewildered that Nicaragua now has 21 movie theaters, when on the eve of the country's revolution in 1979 there were 136. And José is confused when leaders of his party, the Sandinista Front for National Liberation (FSLN), say that the party "remains revolutionary, but in the modern sense of the word." He asks, "What does that mean?"

Like many talented young Nicaraguans of his generation, José entrusted twenty years of his life, his youth and more, to a politically charged set of ideals: revolution, equality, progress, and socialism. Now his memories are unsettling, disorienting, and bizarre. Aside from its abject poverty, Nicaragua shows next to no sign of its traumatic revolution. José's memento is a thick, heavy winter coat he used to wear when in the Soviet Union, completely useless in Nicaragua's tropical heat. José's past, and his present efforts to fit into the Nicaragua that has emerged out of what he helped create, are symptomatic for many in the country, and even for many throughout Latin America at large: the best decades of life are seen as having been spent futilely—even, sometimes, ridiculously—in a protracted political struggle, but nonetheless there are no regrets. Remorse is absent because the prevailing intellectual climate, so it is commonly felt, persuasively dictated the choices made.

José grew up in the provincial capital of Chontales, a dry region in the center of Nicaragua, known for its cattle and cowboys. His mother taught elementary school, and his father drove a tractor; together they raised nine children. Through his aptitude and sheer fortune, José won a scholarship to study in Chile during the turbulent years of Salvador Allende's effort to build socialism. Arriving in 1972, he participated along with nearly every other university student in Chile's political struggles, intellectually and ideologically excited by the vogue for radical change. With the coup d'état, led by General Augusto Pinochet, José was arrested, jailed for four months, always fearful for his life.

Within a year of his return to Nicaragua, José entered the outlawed FSLN. The FSLN was founded by nine young men in 1961, taking as their example—and inspiration—the success of Fidel Castro, Ernesto "Che" Guevara, and other revolutionaries who ousted the Cuban dictator Fulgencio Batista in 1959. Over the years, the FSLN suffered innumerable setbacks, but the clandestine organization was always able to enlist new recruits in their bid to oust the dictatorship of the Somoza family. José was one such recruit. From 1975 to 1977, José was publicly active, protesting against the Somoza regime, until his hidden Sandinista identity was "compromised." He went underground, spending most of the next two years smuggling arms from Panama to Nicaragua. In the final months of the insurrection, José fought in the north of Nicaragua, narrowly surviving a frightful ambush.

With the toppling of Anastasio Somoza in July of 1979, José entered the "police," the Ministry of the Interior, where he came to be third or fourth in rank, and one of the country's most powerful Sandinistas. For most of the years of the revolution, the entry to the headquarters of the Ministry of the Interior (MINT) was adorned with a huge slogan, "The Center of Happiness in Nicaragua." But the ministry was where coercion was dealt out to the perceived enemies of the revolution. And today José readily admits that it was not pleasant.

There were many enemies, because José and his colleagues wanted more than just the ouster of Somoza and the destruction of his hated "national guard." The Sandinistas, nearly all young, were politically intoxicated by the vision of socialism. That vision, powerful as it was, remained vague and tempered by national realities, but carried with it a framework for organizing the state and for state management of the economy. A loose blueprint for institution building and for policy formulation came from countries with "real, existing socialism."

Nicaragua's Ministry of the Interior received guidance and technical assistance from the German Democratic Republic and the Soviet Union, and in the decade of Sandinista rule José made seven or eight trips to the Soviet Union, as well as trips to Cuba, East Germany, Hungary, and Bulgaria. In 1982, during his second or third trip to the Soviet Union (he does not remember which), José suffered a horrible accident. He was traveling in a military convoy in the Ukraine with Soviet army personnel and three other ranking Sandinistas, including *Comandante de la Revolución* Tomás Borge, minister of the interior. The vehicle José was traveling in fell behind, and was hit by a big truck hauling artillery. The other Nicaraguan (on his first trip outside of Nicaragua) in the vehicle was killed, as were three Soviet officers. Only the chauffeur and José survived. But José was left in a body cast from his toes to his armpits, with seventeen pins in his shattered bones.

For four months José lay in an isolated hospital, immobile, cold, in pain, and without a single soul with whom to converse. He spoke no Russian, and no one spoke Spanish. After a month he persuaded his nurse, through sign language, to find him something to read in Spanish: "a history of Soviet patriotic battles." He memorized the elephantine book.

After four months he persuaded another nurse, again through sign language, to wheel his hospital bed to a telephone, where he called the Nicaraguan ambassador in Moscow. After cursing the ambassador for never visiting or calling him, José demanded to be moved, saying that if the ambassador did not move him, he would, on his own, one way or another, leave the hospital and find his way home. The ambassador claimed that there was no hospital in Nicaragua that could attend José given the gravity of his injuries. José's retort was, "Send me somewhere Spanish is spoken."

Shortly thereafter, José—still in his body cast—was on a hellish flight to Cuba. After a miserable, but improved, month in Havana, José returned to Managua, where he spent the last three of his eight months in the same body cast. He returned to Havana to have the cast removed and to begin a rehabilitation program he describes as "pure torture."

After his fifteen months of incapacitation, José returned to the Ministry of Interior. There he worked with two of his brothers, who also held ranking positions. Their native province of Chontales experienced some of the worst, some say the worst, fighting between the Sandinistas and the counterrevolution, the *contra* as it was called then and "the resistance" as it is called now. José does not say much about what he did, either in Managua or in Chontales, other than to say that it was difficult and that mistakes were made. Those with the *contra* say soberly that he was hard (*duro*). Whatever he did, it clearly weighs on him with an eerie solemnity. Yet there is no doubt that he earnestly believed that what he was doing was right. Indeed, given the logic of the paradigm dominant among young intellectuals of his generation in Latin America, what he did not only seemed right; it seemed historically inevitable.

José was in East Berlin a month before the Wall collapsed. He recalls no sign of what was to befall a perceived success, a model. The fall of the Wall, and all that came with it, was a surprise and profoundly disorienting. In Nicaragua itself, a decade of Sandinista rule had revealed problems, even "contradictions," but nothing—it was argued within the FSLN—that an end to United States aggression and "revolutionary discipline" could not solve. His party's loss in the February 1990 elections was devastating and, again, disorienting.

For two more years, José held on to his job as *comandante* at the Ministry of Interior, now called the Ministry of Governance. But work lost its glory and perceived importance. Worse, José was ostracized by the new government. An evening of excitement came in 1992 with the visit of a delegation of United States military personnel. At the conclusion of a long day of tense meetings, José suggested that they "break the ice and come over to his house for drinks." After a few shots of Nicaragua's Flor de Caña rum, each side told its secrets: what was the United States military's plan for invading Nicaragua and what was the Sandinistas' plan for defense from the invasion. Shortly thereafter, José was ousted. The timing of his departure suggests to him that he was ousted because of pressure from the United States Department of State. At least he did negotiate a generous severance agreement. Still, after two decades of commitment to what he views as the most noble and unselfish ideals of his generation, José has a rickety body, a memory of a dreadful accident and a dreary recovery in the most foreign of environments for a Nicaraguan, memories of the death in combat of many of his friends and comrades, a consciousness of having done things that hurt others, political confusion, an impoverished country—and a brand new Mitsubishi Montero (I never asked how he came about the latter).

Ironically, José and his brothers now are committed to the most typical of occupations for folk from Chontales—raising cattle, trying to build up a ranch and a small slaughterhouse. Grand meetings in Moscow have been replaced by harangues about the price of the odd steer. José is now doing just what he would have been doing if socialism, in the end a European political tradition, had never caught the political imagination of the most talented and socially responsible Nicaraguan youth. It is stunning how little remains materially from what was a passionate and all-consuming enterprise.

In Managua itself, the only visible sign of the revolution is an immense, ugly, metal sculpture of a man holding a pick in one arm and a Soviet AK-47 assault rifle in the other. The base of the sculpture proclaims, "Only the peasants and the workers will make it to the end." With Nicaragua now the poorest country in Latin America after Haiti, with unemployment and underemployment at an estimated 50 percent, and with wages for the employed sorely depressed, the sculpture arouses only anger among those it pretends to inspire. (Indeed, someone planted a small bomb that blew off part of one of the figure's feet.)

José's life and the recent history of Nicaragua are emblematic. In Latin America this past century there were four revolutions: Mexico 1910, Bolivia 1952, Cuba 1959, and Nicaragua 1979. Postrevolutionary regimes in Mexico and Bolivia were at least in a limited fashion influenced by the anticapitalist rhetoric of socialism and the oblique but compelling example of the Soviet Union (with such policies as nationalization of the "commanding heights" of industry and organization of peasants into cooperatives). The leaders of the Cuban and Nicaraguan Revolutions were well versed in socialist ideology, and the regimes they crafted in the aftermath of seizing power were more overtly and more decisively modeled on prevailing examples of socialism. Of course, Cuba and Nicaragua are but two small countries in Latin America.

In the second half of this century, though, nearly all countries in Latin America suffered from what the Mexican intellectual Jorge Castañeda has called the "thirty years war": an uneven battle between guerrilla organizations driven by a zeal for socialism and the police and armed forces committed to "law and order." The thirty-year war began in 1959 with the Cuban Revolution, and it ended in 1989 with the collapse of the socialist regimes in Eastern Europe. Most of the casualties of the war were young and on one side. As the Mexican journalist Alma Guillermoprieto commented in an essay published in the October 6, 1997, issue of *The New Yorker*:

> So many incinerated lives: the would-be guerrillas who starved to death in northern Argentina, the young men drowned in vats of excrement in Brazil, the eviscerated martyrs of Guatemala, the sociology student in Argentina whose severed hands were delivered in a jar to her mother: The children of Che [Guevara]. The slogans that defined those furious and hopeful times "The first duty of a revolutionary is to make the Revolution." . . . sound foolish and empty now, but . . . they were heard and followed.

Those, such as José Figueroa, who survived this thirty-year war had their lives thoroughly disrupted.

But this war generated more than casualties. It spawned passionate ideas about how to govern society and how to modernize economies. The decimation of guerrilla groups in so many countries and the sorry fate of revolutionary regimes in Nicaragua and Cuba distort how the ideas associated with socialism often shaped policy formulation and implementation in Latin America. One of the most persuasive ideas was that trade with powerful capitalist countries was harmful; local industry had to be fostered so that imports could be substituted for locally produced goods. There were subsidies for national firms, barriers to foreign investment, high tariffs, and even state industries. A more general idea was simply that the state should have a prominent role in the economy. These ideas were embraced by the Chilean regime of Salvador Allende, a self-proclaimed socialist who came to power in a democratic election. They were embraced, too, by "left-leaning" military officers in Peru who staged a coup in 1968 and ushered in many reforms designed to remake Peru. Yet, versions of some of these same "statist" policies were also embraced by "right-wing" military officers in Brazil, who, after ousting a left-leaning president (in 1964), built large and powerful state enterprises and developed extensive state control over the world's tenth largest economy.

More generally, the struggle between the "left" and the "right" generated an intellectual debate that asked probing questions about economic development, inequality, poverty, social responsibility, and the obligations of the state. Universities in particular were inflamed, but so were labor unions and movements, political parties, the Catholic Church, and even, admittedly to a lesser degree, organizations of the private sector. Answers to searching questions were elusive, but issues were at least addressed. No government was immune to this heady debate and the demands it generated for solutions to economic stagnation, inequality, and poverty.

The collapse of socialism as an ideal cannot be pinned to a particular date. It was teetering before 1989, when the socialist regimes of Eastern Europe collapsed. But the end in 1991 of the Soviet Union, the fatherland of Lenin, was decisive for the "left" in Latin America. Surviving guerrilla organizations, including prominently Sendero Luminoso in Peru, suddenly seemed not just politically untenable, but decidedly anachronistic. And the collapse of socialism weakened faith in the ability of the state to guide judiciously economic development. Evidence had been accumulating that the state bureaucracies of Latin America were grossly inefficient, and that state intervention in markets was often pernicious. But suddenly there was no longer even a rationale for the state to assume economic responsibilities. Socialism had been the one ideology that had collected disparate concerns about poverty and inequality, offered an explanation for their continued presence, and promised a just redistribution of wealth and a future of equitable economic growth. With the end of socialism, there appeared—even to erstwhile revolutionaries like José Figueroa—no alternative to liberal democracy and to its handmaiden, capitalism. Concomitantly, there appeared no bold solution to the poverty and inequality of Latin America. Utopia vanished, and with it went political activism.

Aside from poverty, the legacy of the Sandinista Revolution is the political organization of every group with a shared interest. Even ex-members of the *contra* have organized themselves to get their entitlements from a fragile and bankrupt state. But if Nicaragua is replete with organizations, including the country's twenty-three political parties, it is not clear to thoughtful Nicaraguans what to believe in other than self-interest. And most political debates turn out to be, upon close examination, little more than struggles over resources. The Sandinistas were replaced by the administration of Violeta Barrios de Chamorro, who ruled without a party. She was committed to healing the wound in what she referred to as the "Nicaraguan family." Violeta Barrios was succeeded, in turn, by Arnoldo Alemán. He did come to power with the support of a political party, the Nationalist Liberal Party (PLN)—the political party of the Somoza family—but just what the party stands for today remains vague. (In July 2000, I interviewed the president of the party, Leopoldo Navarro; he said the party is committed to "liberalism.") To be sure, there is—in Nicaragua and just about everywhere else in Latin America—a commitment to democracy and to markets, but it is a commitment without passion. It is as if there is democracy and markets by default; nothing else exists. There is a bankruptcy of political and economic models, and even, perhaps, a fatigue with exploring searching political questions.

José has retreated from politics. He continues to be loyal to his party, still Nicaragua's strongest political party, but he is no longer sure what it means to be a Sandinista. His ties to the FSLN are mostly ones of friendship. But José is well aware that the FSLN has been weakened by divisions between its leaders. José has stayed loyal to the head of the party, and the head of Nicaragua's government from 1979 to 1990, Daniel Ortega. Further turmoil to the FSLN came with accusations in 1998 by Ortega's stepdaughter, Zoilamérica, that he sexually abused her for years, beginning when she was eleven. I asked José what he thought of the accusation. He was quiet for a moment but finally said, firmly, "When I knew Daniel Ortega it was as a fellow combatant and he was a model of ethical behavior."

José keeps his boots clean and looks after his cattle.

# Chapter 5

## Fragile Democracies

I ASKED a young Brazilian in Rio de Janeiro how President Fernando Henrique Cardoso was doing. "Oh, he is doing fine." A pause. "It is the rest of us who are not doing so well." This beguiling response can serve as a leitmotiv for how many Latin Americans view their new democratic regimes. It has just been a few years since authoritarian regimes— mostly military-led—were replaced with popularly elected, civilian governments throughout the region. These new regimes have survived. But the fanfare and enthusiasm that marked the transition have given way to a more guarded view of democractic governance in the region, and, indeed, to increasing cynicism and apathy. Much can be said about the state of democracy in Latin America, but ten succinct ideas can help explain this disappointment and suggest what it might imply for the future of democracy in the region.

The 1980s in Latin America have been dismissed as a "lost decade," in response to a continentwide economic recession of proportions not seen since the 1930s. In some countries, real per capita income fell by as much as 25 percent. Politically, though, the decade was anything but "lost": the predominance of authoritarian rule in the 1960s and 1970s gave way to an unanticipated wave of "democratization." Celebrations greeted the emergence, in country after country, of constitutional rule, competitive party politics, and civilian supremacy. The world at large was impressed with images of long lines of poor peasants, in countries such as El Salvador, walking kilometers to exercise their right to vote.

The first Latin American country to restore democratic institutions was Ecuador, in 1979. It was followed by its neighbor Peru in 1980, Argentina in 1983, and Uruguay in 1984. In Central America, the militaries returned to the barracks in El Salvador in 1984 and in Guatemala in 1986. In 1989 Brazil finally broke free from a military regime that had begun in 1964. Dating the transition in Bolivia and in Honduras is more difficult, but in both countries 1985 seems to have been a pivotal year. Two of the last countries to join the fashionable embracing of democracy, in 1990, were countries with an experience of "socialism," Chile and Nicaragua. Paraguay closed the cycle with its open and competitive elections in 1993 (some Paraguayans date their transition to the elections of 1989 even though the victor was a general who had a few months earlier overthrown the dictator Alfredo Stroessner). These new democracies joined the three countries where democratic processes had been established earlier: Costa Rica (1948), Colombia (1958), and Venezuela (1958).

As can be expected with such a diverse group of countries, there are many degrees of "success" with democracy. Countries that appear more successful include Chile, Uruguay, Bolivia, Argentina, El Salvador, and

Costa Rica. On the other end of the continuum are Peru, Ecuador, Venezuela, Brazil, Honduras, and Nicaragua. Differing outcomes are not easy to explain. There is no correlation between those countries that embraced democracy "early" or "late" and the initial set of outcomes of that transition. Peru, for example, was one of the first countries to return to civilian rule, and its governance remains most problematic. Brazil was one of the last countries to embark on democratic rule, and it, too, is problematic. Similarly, there is no easy correlation between the depth of earlier political conflict and present stability. Bolivia, for example, has a history of extreme political instability—characterized by military coups d'état—yet today it seems stable. Venezuela has a history of constitutional rule, but it is floundering. Surprisingly, there are no socioeconomic indicators, such as per capita income, that predict political outcomes.

Certain generalizations, however, can be made for Latin America as a whole.

1. *A number of indicators suggest that both new and old democratic regimes are under stress, their legitimacy is being questioned, and their public support is increasingly fragile.* Public opinion polls in individual countries, and for the region as a whole, demonstrate declining public confidence in democracy. A comprehensive survey of attitudes on government and politics in seventeen Latin American countries, undertaken in 1996 by a private polling organization based in Chile, Barómetro Latinoamericano, showed only a minority of those polled expressing satisfaction with the performance of their country's democracy. The same frustration—or disappointment—was registered in polls conducted by Latinobarómetro in 1997 and 1998. Support for the performance of democratic regimes is highest in Uruguay and Costa Rica, and lowest in such countries as Brazil, Paraguay, Ecuador, and Honduras. The sweeping conclusion from the 1998 polling was that only 35 percent of Latin Americans are satisfied with the performance of their democracy. Public opinion polls also suggest widespread disappointment with the institutions of democracy, in particular with legislatures and political parties.

Also indicative of the fragility of democracy in Latin America is the declining voter turnout in elections. In Brazil, for example, voting is obligatory, yet in the 1998 presidential elections, 36 percent of the 106 million Brazilians eligible to vote stayed home or cast blank or invalid votes. Fernando Henrique Cardoso was reelected president by only 34 percent of the total voting population. In Colombia, abstention has climbed to over 50 percent. In Guatemala's 1996 presidential elections, in the departments of Huehuetenango and Quiché, where the population is overwhelmingly indigenous, 74 percent of eligible voters stayed home. In the country's 1999 national referendum, the abstention rate was 81 percent. After approving a new constitution in 1999, Venezuelans voted in 2000 in two rounds of "mega-elections": in the first election—for national, state, and municipal posts—the turnout was only 55 percent; in the second election—for more local posts—the turnout fell to 23 percent.

Another disturbing indicator is the lack of support offered to candidates of traditional political parties. In some countries, such as Peru and Venezuela, important parties have all but collapsed. Alternatively, candidates with no political experience have won elections. Alberto Fujimori in Peru is the best-known case. There also appears to be an increasing tendency—accepted by the public—to concentrate power in the executive, who rules by decrees instead of by laws. Finally, many in the media and the academic community openly express doubts about the desirability of democracy. They talk of the "Pinochet model," a "democracy of low intensity," and of a "façade of democracy."

What is happening? Why the declining support for democracy so soon after the scandals of "dirty wars," "*los desaparecidos*," and incompetent economic management by befuddled generals?

2. *Public dissatisfaction is not directed at the economic model of the day, unfettered markets.* Instead, public disenchantment is focused on corruption and ineptitude in governing. A regionwide survey of public attitudes by the Spanish magazine *Cambio 16* revealed that for the overwhelming majority the most serious problem in their countries is corruption. In impoverished Bolivia, for example, most Bolivians say that corruption is a more serious problem than unemployment. Election results also do not demonstrate public rejection of the liberal economic model. Wealthy businessmen with programs of economic liberalization win elections, for example, Juan Carlos Wasmosy in Paraguay. In the 1993 Chilean election, 90 percent of the votes went to candidates who accepted the reigning economic model. Even the 1998 election in Venezuela of Hugo Chávez—a former army colonel and coup plotter—can be interpreted not as a vote against liberalism, but instead a vote against corruption in the country's traditional political parties. The dominant attitude in the region is best captured by a Mexican intellectual who said he no longer cared about governments of the right or the left; he would settle for any *honest* government.

The 1999 presidential elections in Argentina are illuminating. From 1989 to 1999, President Carlos Menem revamped Argentina's economy with his singular emphasis on liberal reforms, including extensive privatization and other efforts to reduce the role of the state in the economy. Although his party, the Peronist party, lost the 1999 election, there was no sign that voters wanted a change in economic policy. Instead, exit polls indicated that voters wanted to "send a message," rejecting Menem's flamboyant lifestyle and perceptions that he tolerated corrupt officials in his administration. Exit polls also showed that voters perceived the victor, Fernando de la Rúa, to be honest. Only a third of his voters reported casting their ballot for him because of his policy proposals, which, in any case, did not break with President Menem's economic reforms.

3. *The public has sweeping (and perhaps unfair) criteria for granting political legitimacy.* Intellectuals may separate regime type from everyday public administration, but the public makes no such distinction. Legitimacy is accorded to governors not on the basis of how they acquired power, but of what they do with it. The abrupt transition from authoritarianism to democracy in the 1980s was not accompanied by a wholesale remaking of the bureaucracies that provide (or do not provide) all-important services to a needy public. In too many instances, the state remains inefficient, unresponsive, and corrupt. Costa Rica has been a democracy since 1948, but a bumper sticker suggests the challenge facing winners of elections in Latin America: "Every time I hit a pothole, I think of the president." In neighboring Nicaragua, a leader of Congress told me that a survey of Nicaraguans revealed that the expectation of members of Congress is that they help secure jobs and visas to the United States. Throughout Latin America, there is a need not just to improve the machinery of government, but also to explain what are reasonable expectations of government—and democratic government in particular. The Uruguayan statesman Julio María Sanguinetti, goes further, suggesting that democracy demands a supportive political culture. As he puts it, in the most telling of phraseology, "Consumers need to be citizens, too."

4. *Political parties are the weakest link in Latin America's democracies.* In contemporary democractic theory, political parties are the essential building blocks. They have responsibility for aggregating public preferences, formulating plans for governing, and fielding candidates. With only limited exceptions, political parties in Latin America are not institutionalized, they are not stable, they do not have roots in society, they are not independent of ambitious leaders, and they are not democratic in their internal organization. In the aftermath of military rule in Ecuador, the country has seemingly made a habit of each time electing a president from a different political party. Between fourteen and seventeen parties routinely compete in legislative elections, with at least ten of them winning seats. The strongest party in Congress at any one time has never represented anything close to a majority of voters, polling between 15 and 30 percent of the vote, and usually about 20 percent. None of Ecuador's political parties has deep roots in society. Indeed,

even politicians have shallow roots in their own political parties. One of the features of Ecuador's politics is what is called *cambio de camiseta* (change of shirt): candidates for positions in Congress run for election under a party banner, but once elected they commonly change parties, or just proclaim themselves independents. At times, more than a fourth of the members of Congress claim no party affiliation. Party affiliation is shed so as to enhance the bargaining power of individual members of Congress. I asked an Ecuadorian congressman, in the privacy of his office, how much a congressional vote was worth. "If it is not a vote of great importance, something like two jobs in the customs authority."

Other countries, notably Brazil, also suffer from political fragmentation. Brazil has twenty political parties; so everything depends on "coalitions." And the stability of coalitions is continually undermined by members of Congress changing parties at will. Even in regimes that are essentially two-party systems, such as Honduras, there are no strong connections between society and party. Electoral competition has not been sufficient to end cronyism, indifference, and corruption. In Honduras, public sentiment toward the country's two political parties is captured by the quip: "They eat from the same plate." In the Dominican Republic there is an even more disturbing maxim about the country's political elite: "They are white and they understand one another." Much work still needs to be done to improve the responsiveness and public accountability of Latin America's political parties if elections are to become more meaningful and confer more legitimacy.

5. *The reform of political parties is stymied by a lack of political involvement on the part of many of the middle class, of the managers and professionals whose skills are sorely needed.* Throughout the region there is a common fatalism about politics, as if all outcomes are foreordained. Political parties are left to *políticos*. As a Guatemalan manager put it, "*Los buenos no se meten*" (Decent people do not get involved). This lack of political participation in the management of political parties, and in politics in general, is at odds with common ideas about the economy, which is held to need constant scrutiny and calibration. A similar attitude toward politics is lacking.

6. *Political participation is retarded in part by the lack of ideas, of conflicting paradigms on how best to organize state and society.* As a member of Venezuela's Congress put it, "There is no debate because there are no alternatives." A Peruvian journalist, Raúl Wiener, has argued that Peruvian politics has suffered from "a general crisis of intellectual production." It is telling—and depressing, too—that no one reads anymore. Before, those on the left were the most studious, the most inclined to read political theory. But now they do not read, not Marx, not Lenin, and not any substitutes. A former guerrilla in El Sal-

vador, now a member of the Democratic Party (PD), told me: "There is nothing to read; there are no reference points." For her and her colleagues, one learns only from the experience of governing.

The silence of intellectuals and politicians is striking. They both are terribly short of ideals that can mobilize people. In particular, there is little evidence of energy and creativity in searching for ways in which state and society can ameliorate inequality and poverty. Innovation in public administration is largely confined to public finance, where the guiding aspiration is inevitably to rein in government spending (and so avoid inflation-spawning deficits). Private initiatives are few. The poor are seen as an inevitable part of the social landscape.

Even Latin America's last guerrillas, those of Colombia, are seemingly bereft of ideas. Guerrillas operate in nearly half of Colombia and control a sizable part of the country. They are fought by the military and by paramilitary forces. The fighting is savage and has generated a major social crisis. But what is the fighting about? The largest rebel group is the Revolutionary Armed Forces of Colombia (FARC). What, if anything, does it advocate? It has not articulated an ideology or a set of proposals, leaving it open to charges that it fights for the spoils of the trade in narcotics and the gains from such crimes as kidnapping. The FARC has not contributed to political debate in Colombia, let alone elsewhere in Latin America. A Colombian executive, who travels frequently throughout the country, told me the fighting in Colombia—or the war as she labeled it—will not be easily resolved, because of "*intereses*" (interests). I asked her what did she mean by *intereses*. "Money."

7. *In the absence of ideas—and of passions—there are only interests.* These, of course, have always existed. But perhaps they are more transparent now. Latin America has always been characterized as being both more culturally homogeneous and more radically inegalitarian than other parts of the world. In fact, inequality is real enough, homogeneity less so. The ethnic schism between indigenous people and those referred to as *ladinos* is pronounced. Indigenous populations are better organized and more independent today, especially in countries where they constitute a substantial part of the population. Afro-Brazilians—who represent perhaps 40 percent of the population of Brazil—are also increasingly able to make demands for a redress in their subordinate status.

There are now more pronounced—and growing—divisions, not based on ethnicity, but rather between the capital and the rest of the country (the "interior" as it is still sometimes called in Havana). The economic and cultural disparities between the capital and the remainder of the country introduce an odd disjunct into the politics of representation. In Guatemala, for example, it can be argued that the winner of the

1996 presidential election was the candidate of Guatemala City; the loser was the candidate of the rest of the country. Increasingly, the route to the presidency in Latin America includes serving as mayor of the capital.

In some countries regional disparities are pronounced. The wealthiest state in Mexico, Nueva León (located in the north), has a per capita income ten times that of the poorest Mexican state, Chiapas (located in the south). In a number of countries, including Colombia, Ecuador, Peru, and Bolivia, there is a rivalry between the *sierra* and the lowlands. (Ecuadorians from the *sierra* call their brethren on the coast "monkeys.") It remains to be seen how ethnic, regional, and urban-rural divisions will play themselves out, as they do complicate the aggregation of interests, but the basic political fault lines are becoming decidedly less ideological.

8. *In the fragile democracies of Latin America, the political risk is not, as in decades past, of a return to military rule.* The military realizes that the international context has changed and that the pressures on anyone seeking to usurp power would be overwhelming. In any case, the soldiers have no inclination to govern. There are no visible dangers to either the nation or their own prerogatives. Like so many others today in Latin America, ranking military officers are interested in making money. Many officers, throughout the region, have business interests on the side. And the military as an institution often owns and operates businesses, sometimes of an ominous kind, such as the cemetery run by the armed forces in Honduras.

Instead, the greater political danger to democracy in Latin America comes from a growing number of voters who either abstain from voting altogether or vote for antidemocratic candidates who offer "simple solutions" to complex problems. "Simple solutions" are a populist mantra. Populism in Latin America is an elastic concept, but it is most commonly associated with redistributive economic policies, usually financed in an unsustainable manner. Populism has a less well-understood political dimension, however: the "politics of antipolitics." Populists who come to power via democratic elections govern in an authoritarian style justified by continual attacks on traditional political elites and established institutions.

Today, economic populism is not the threat it was in earlier decades. There has been considerable "economic learning" by elites, including those of the private sector and governmental bureaucracies, and the international financial community is always on guard. A political leader bent on pursuing populist economic policies would quickly confront opposition from a daunting coalition of institutionalized actors who can put unbearable pressure on any maverick leader.

Much more likely, today, are forms of political populism à la Alberto Fujimori—antiparty politics. Alberto Fujimori, the son of Japanese immigrants, assumed the presidency of Peru in 1990 after winning a competitive election. But he augmented his power in 1992 by what is now known throughout Latin America as a *fujimorazo*—dissolving Congress under the pretext that legislators were corrupt and inept. Democracy's "checks and balances" were dismantled with the argument that public faith in Peru's traditional political parties had declined. Fujimori offered "administration," not "politics." Surely, all Peruvians recognized that this gambit was antidemocratic. Nonetheless, in Peru—and elsewhere in Latin America—voters can become so frustrated with the traditional parties that they opt for exciting if dangerous leaders. Even elites, fearful of economic populism, may acquiesce in a political leadership that is determined to *govern*. But this kind of heady and combative government inevitably contributes to the further weakening of democratic institutions, including political parties, legislatures, and the judiciary. Thus, the important question for Peru is not how well or badly Alberto Fujimori governed, but whether anyone can govern Peru in the aftermath of his clumsy exit from the presidency—and Peru—in November 2000.

9. *The democracies of Latin America are hostage to economic trends and are vulnerable to economic shocks.* There is statistical evidence that the percentage of poor people in Chile has declined because of robust economic growth, up to an enviable 6 percent to 8 percent per year. In Costa Rica, the successful promotion of exports and the development of tourism have resulted in a low unemployment rate. In many other countries, though, the "new" economic strategy has brought painful dislocations, such as the surge in unemployment in Argentina. And there is scattered but persuasive evidence that economic liberalization and the development of new export commodities are exacerbating inequality. These unequal gains—or losses, as the case may be—translate into political tensions. For example, in El Salvador, the political party National Republican Alliance (ARENA) is threatened with fragmentation because of divisions between the agro-export elite, who founded the party but are not faring so well, and the financial-sector elite, who increasingly dominate the party. Shifts in economic policies bring sharp and sudden shifts in economic fortunes. Resilient democracies can cope, but can fragile democracies?

Another, more nettlesome question: How dependent has Latin America become on a healthy world economy, and, in particular, on capital inflows? For a number of years Latin America has had a very large capital inflow, billions of dollars annually. This investment, along with healthy markets for many of the region's exports, has caused a spurt of economic growth and patched over many problems—including increased inequality. What happens if capital dries up, or if world trade contracts? The economic difficulties in Latin America during the 1980s were exacerbated by indebtedness. Latin American countries continue to have considerable foreign debt, which is constraining and which makes the region especially vulnerable to a contraction in the world economy. There is an expression in financial circles: When the United States sneezes, Europe gets a cold. Perhaps the corollary is, and Latin America gets pneumonia.

10. *Mexico may be a bellwether rather than an exception.* In Latin America there is an expression, "*Como México no hay dos*" (There is no place like Mexico). Mexico is sui generis. Before the wave of democracy in Latin America, Mexico did not look so bad: the military was nowhere to be seen, there were elections, and there was a periodic change of presidents. After the "transitions" elsewhere, though, Mexico looked like what the Peruvian writer Mario Vargas Llosa labeled it, "the perfect dictatorship." Elections and a new president every six years no longer masked the fact that the country was essentially a one-party state, the kingdom of the Institutional Revolutionary Party (PRI), founded in 1929. The party mixed paternalistic populism with electoral skulduggery to become the longest-ruling political party in the world.

The PRI provided a façade of legitimacy for cronyism, clientelism, and corruption. The 1982 economic crisis in Mexico stimulated some effort at political reform, as did—again—the 1994 crisis. Although the leadership of the PRI sometimes gave the impression that its attitude was "things have to change so that nothing changes," a variety of circumstances and some statesmanship led to elections in 2000 that were free and competitive. And the PRI lost.

The candidate of the National Action Party (PAN), Vicente Fox, won the election. His campaign appearances included his stomping a plastic dinosaur, representing the PRI, with his cowboy boots. In Fox's December 2000 inauguration address to Congress, he promised there would be, after seventy-one years of continuity, "a new political future," with a "reform of the state, breaking paradigms." But is a new "paradigm" for governing truly in the offering?

Mexican voters, cynical though they were for decades about the PRI, are partly responsible for the party's long hold on power. Throughout Mexico there was a fear of change, of leaping into the unknown, perhaps from the historical memory of the costs of the Mexican Revolution, which had been a succession of bloody civil wars. Seven percent of the population lost their lives, and economic growth did not resume for twenty years. So a premium was for a long time put on stability. Mexicans voted for an alternative to the PRI only when it was safe to do so, when there was an end to ideological differences that might reverberate throughout state and society. Conflict is being averted, but so is the possibility of profound change. A Mexican president who is not from the PRI is now a threat only to the cronyism of the PRI. Mexico is different, in so many ways, from the rest of Latin America; yet politically Mexico enters the twenty-first century with the same absence of ideological—and thus programmatic—contestation that is lacking elsewhere.

In sum, Latin America's democracies are not in danger of collapse right now. There are many real problems, though, and not many indications that these problems are being addressed with imagination and determination. It is not clear how tired and cynical voters will react if further deterioration takes place, or if the region is subjected to economic shocks. True, the region's democracies have brought peace and greater protection of basic human rights. Democratic governments have brought a welcome sense of "normalcy," too. What is notable, though, is not just that the democracies are "rickety," hardly prepared to tackle difficult economic and social problems, but that the populace is not prepared to engage in deep discussions about state and society, about needs and aspirations, and about how these needs and aspirations could be met. The considerable promises of democracy have yet to be fulfilled in Latin America.

# Chapter 6

## The Business of Being in Business

GILBERTO ESCOBAR was working in one of Ecuador's largest sugar refineries in 1979, but he was keeping an eye on the development of shrimp farms in the shallow Bay of Guayaquil. In the marshy littoral of the bay a hectare of land jumped from eight dollars to two hundred dollars in just eight months. Gilberto left his position at the sugar refinery and began to buy land. When he began his life as an entrepreneur, or as is said in Spanish, *un hombre de negocios* (a man of business), his net worth, by his own calculation, was $60,000. But of that sum $27,000 was tied up in a vehicle. Only $25,000 was "cash." Nonetheless, he bought one hundred hectares of land and began to make the necessary investments to be able to cultivate shrimp. He had to borrow money, which made him nervous.

His first revenue came two years later, in 1981. That year he produced 350,000 pounds of shrimp. He bought more land and increased his production. In 1986 he produced, for export, 2.2 million pounds of shrimp. Gilberto made a lot of money, and he made it quickly. At the time in Ecuador, the profit margin in shrimp was generally held to be 50 percent, which is to say that half of the dollar value of sales could be assumed to be profit. Gilberto enjoyed the best of what was to be had in the muggy city of Guayaquil, including membership in the prestigious Union Club. And he took summer seminars at the Harvard Business School to enrich himself, and he traveled to Europe to enjoy himself.

The spectacular success of Gilberto was shared. The first intent to cultivate shrimp in Ecuador was in 1968, but commercial production did not begin until 1977. A decade later, Ecuador was one of the principal exporters of shrimp in the world. More than 133,000 hectares of land were dedicated to the cultivation of shrimp, 80 percent of which was in the area surrounding the shallow Bay of Guayaquil. Shrimp exports in 1982 totaled $122 million and in 1992 reached $526 million. An estimated 200,000 Ecuadorians were employed in the industry.

Even Ecuador's armed forces entered the business. Close to Gilberto's shrimp pools were pools owned and operated by the military. The "logic" of the military producing shrimp eluded Gilberto. As he passed their pools in his boat he sometimes wondered if the recruits who labored at the pools were paid by the government, if the enterprise paid taxes, and just who pocketed the profits of the business. (But he never stopped to ask any questions.)

While Ecuador's exports of shrimp in 1992 appeared strong, especially in comparison with 1982, a serious problem emerged in the sector: mortality rates for cultivated shrimp began to soar. Some loss of shrimp is normal and so expected. But in the Bay of Guayaquil the mortality rate soared, with considerable variation among producers. Local and foreign scientists looked for bacteria or a virus. Nothing was found. Forms of pollution were examined, too. Nothing turned up until someone looked at the importation of chemicals into Ecuador to see if anything correlated with the onset of problems in the shrimp industry. A correlation did emerge: the importation of new fungicides for the banana industry was shortly followed by the abrupt rise in shrimp morality.

Suspicion increasingly focused on the banana industry. In 1991 a deadly fungus, Sigatoka Negra, appeared in the north of the country. By 1992 the fungus had spread to the principal areas of banana cultivation in the country. Banana producers responded with the use of different fungicides, the three most common being Tilt, Calixin, and Benlate. Ninety percent of the rivers that drain the banana-producing zone empty into the Bay of Guayaquil. Moreover, it was observed that shrimp mortality was highest in the rainy season, when the use of the banana fungicides was also greatest.

The abnormal mortality of shrimp came to be known as the "Taura syndrome." (Taura is the name of one of the rivers that drains into the Bay of Guayaquil.) Certainty of the origin of the plague was increased when scientists conducted controlled experiments on the coast. In those tanks where banana fungicides were added, shrimp mortality climbed, with dying and dead shrimp having the same characteristics associated with the Taura syndrome. But in those tanks where no fungicides were added, mortality rates were normal. Still, no explanation was found as to how the fungicides killed shrimp. Correlation, not causation, was established.

In 1993 additional shrimp pools were affected by the Taura syndrome. Producers began to panic. For Gilberto, every six-month cycle of shrimp cultivation required an investment of $1.5 million. His production—and so his earnings—fell considerably in the first half of 1993. Gilberto decided not to invest in a second cycle. He laid off two hundred employees, leaving only five guards at the pools and five employees in his office (located in Guayaquil). Bankers were nervous, too. By the end of the year they stopped extending credit to shrimp producers. And many shrimp farmers were reluctant to commit their own capital. At the beginning of 1994, the shrimp industry appeared to be on the verge of collapse.

Efforts to find a solution were thwarted. Banana producers denied responsibility. They said that if shrimp farmers had a problem with their water that they should filter it. They also pointed to the many forms of pollution fouling the Bay of Guayaquil. The city of Guayaquil, for example, which is Ecuador's largest city with a population of more than 1.5 million inhabitants, has no sewage treatment. Sewage is just dumped in the Guayas River, the principal river that empties into the

Bay of Guayaquil. A study prepared in 1996 identified, moreover, 451 industrial firms in the area, many of which released waste materials into the Guayas River or the Bay of Guayaquil. No one could overlook the many sources of pollution in the Bay of Guayaquil, but Gilberto and his fellow shrimp farmers considered the evidence targeting the fungicides of the banana industry as damning. And they noted, too, that not just their shrimp were dying; fish, crabs, and other marine life were abruptly disappearing from the region's rivers and from the Bay of Guayaquil.

The indifference of banana producers led shrimp farmers to seek mediation from the government. Officials were approached, but they were not helpful, apparently for a number of reasons: (1) the government was not convinced of the seriousness of the problem; (2) the government was fragmented, and so, weak; (3) much attention was paid to the economic importance of the banana industry; and (4) no easy solution appeared at hand.

Gilberto resolved to organize shrimp producers and to fight to defend the shrimp industry, and so his livelihood. Logical steps seemed to include strengthening the association of shrimp producers, generating more information about the Taura syndrome (especially from dispassionate scientists), and pressuring the government to identify and implement a solution to resolve the problem generated by the use of the deadly fungicides. Some funds were collected, a public relations firm was hired, scientists were invited to the shrimp farms, and politicians were hounded. Gilberto, who became a spokesman for the industry, was interviewed by newspapers and appeared on television "talk shows" to explain the problem—and point a finger at the culprits. On one of his television appearances, Gilberto managed to show parts of a documentary financed by shrimp producers, in which, for example, planes fumigating banana plantations were observed "spraying" as they passed over bodies of water—and even houses.

In addition to fomenting scientific research, engaging in a public relations campaign, and lobbying the government, shrimp farmers considered filing a lawsuit against the three foreign producers of the fungicides. Not much faith existed, however, in Ecuador's legal system. The resolution of business disputes in Ecuador can take years. Another strategy considered was to contact international ecology organizations and appeal for their help. This strategy, though, was deemed risky. It could damage irrevocably the international market for Ecuador's shrimp. Also, many "environmentalists" were hostile to shrimp farmers because of the mangroves they destroyed when they built their pools.

Despite Gilberto's efforts, shrimp farmers never truly united or pooled their collective resources. There are various explanations for their organizational failure:

1. producers in different locations were unevenly affected by the plague (some suffered a great deal while others were barely touched);
2. there was considerable variation in the size of the shrimp farms, and small producers did not get along with large producers and vice versa;
3. some shrimp farmers were also banana producers and so had conflicts of interest;
4. some producers took advantage of the misfortune of others, buying shrimp farms for 10 percent of their previous value (5 percent of shrimp farmers left the business);
5. personality clashes.

The burden of defending the interests of shrimp farmers fell disproportionately on a few individuals, including prominently Gilberto.

In any case, the government did nothing. The government was weak, in large measure because of a fragmentation of power. The president was of one party; the vice president was from another party. Ten parties were represented in the small, unicameral legislature, with no one party having anything close to a majority. The party of the president had only a marginal presence in Congress. Moreover, the vice president had an interest in a fumigation company (he later abruptly fled the country on the eve of being indicted for corruption). And the minister of agriculture was a banana farmer. Gilberto considered the country's political system "hopeless."

Gilberto concluded that Ecuador had an ugly choice: shrimp or bananas. If banana growers persisted in using their deadly fungicides, the shrimp industry would be lost. But he understood that if the banana industry did not use their fungicides, the banana industry would collapse. The choice was ugly: in 1992 Ecuador exported $648 million worth of bananas and $526 million worth of shrimp. While bananas were Ecuador's second most valuable export (after petroleum), shrimp were a close third. Gilberto believed that shrimp farmers should prevail, that they had the moral high ground, but he realized that the absence of a government capable of administering "justice" meant that the banana industry would dominate. Gilberto thought of moving to East Africa, where ideal conditions were supposed to exist for cultivating shrimp. His wife, however, said she was not leaving Ecuador.

A shock came in November 1994. Scientists in Hawaii discovered that the Taura syndrome was, in fact, a virus. The news was widely reported, including in the newspapers of Ecuador. Banana producers were relieved, and concluded that the discovery of the virus absolved them of any responsibility. Gilberto and his colleagues did not agree with this position; they maintained that the fungicides might well weaken shrimp, leaving them susceptible to the virus. But Gilberto and his colleagues concluded that their plan to file a lawsuit in Florida against the producers of the fungicides was no longer viable.

Back at his farm Gilberto had to make difficult choices. The farm had been closed for some time. But Gilberto had slowly—and cautiously—resumed production. He soon had fifty employees (instead of the two hundred in the "boom years") and five hundred hectares in production. Production was resumed only with the addition of measures to limit shrimp mortality. Some ponds were used just to filter water for ponds containing shrimp. Gilberto used a wild larva that was more resistant to disease, and he reduced the number of shrimp per hectare to thirty thousand (a third to a half of what had previously been the "density"). He also experimented with the cultivation of fish in ten hectares.

Gilberto made some money but not much. He could take a chance and resume production at previous levels. But it was a gamble. The banks were still not extending credit to the shrimp industry. Gilberto had the $1.5 million that he would need to invest for a cycle. If the shrimp died, though, he would be "finished"; he would not have the capital to invest in another cycle or in another business. Neither would he have money to sustain a comfortable retirement.

Gilberto's shrimp farm could only be sold for "ten cents on the dollar," in other words, for 10 percent of its previously established value. So there was no easy "exit," he said, from the business. He could, though, just walk away from it, but that would be "painful." Still, Gilberto realized that he had "to be careful not to become a Don Quixote." He concluded that the golden years of the shrimp business had passed and that he had to concentrate on diversifying his financial interests. Even if, he realized, the virus behind the Taura syndrome was eradicated, a new virus—perhaps from Asia's shrimp industry—could emerge and prove ruinous. Gilberto elected to diversify his financial interests by expanding production of fish in his pools and by developing a mango farm.

The fish Gilberto cultivated was tilapia. Demand seemed strong. And Gilberto concluded that the world's oceans are not going to be able to produce more fish. Catfish, trout, and salmon are being successful produced by what is known as aquaculture. Tilapia is a whitefish that does well in the tropical climate of the Guayaquil region. Pools previously used to cultivate shrimp were turned over to the production of fish.

Concurrently, Gilberto bought one hundred hectares of land and planted mango trees. The site was north of Guayaquil in an area with other "plantations." The expectation was a $10,000 investment per hectare, a total thus of $1 million. But the addition of a drip irrigation system and a packing and refrigeration system added another $500,000 to the investment. Gilberto understood that for four to five years there would only be expenses. In the sixth year of a mango plantation some revenue is expected. Only in the seventh year is there a beginning of a return on the investment.

In the sixth year of Gilberto's mango plantation, just as he was anticipating revenues, problems emerged. On the plantation itself there was a problem of theft and of the difficulties of managing the large, temporal labor force for the harvest. Worse, many in the area had followed Gilberto into the mango business, but without his awareness of the importance of quality. Ecuador's mangoes began to be viewed skeptically in the all-important European market. Premium prices were elusive. Moreover, the Noboa family in Guayaquil had a virtual monopoly on container freight to Europe, and shipping costs were high, eating heavily into profit margins.

In 1997–1998 came an abrupt change of climate caused by the phenomenon known as El Niño. Abnormal fluctuation in sea surface temperatures in the tropical Pacific caused torrential rainfall in Peru and Ecuador. Heavy rains prevented the mango trees from flowering and developing fruit. The 1997–1998 season was a disaster; there were no revenues at all. The mango plantation was now no longer a headache; it was an enormous loss. Gilberto's $1.5 million investment generated only continuing expenses. And it could only be sold for $300,000, if he could find a buyer.

His investment in fish cultivation also soured. The cost of feed doubled while the price for fish dropped; his production costs far exceeded his revenue. Gilberto quit cultivating fish.

Ironically, the heavy rains brought by El Niño were good for the shrimp industry. The heavy rains flushed out pollutants, raised the temperature of the water in the pools, and stimulated the growth of nutrients in the pools. Gilberto wondered, too, if the shrimp industry improved because the foreign producers of the banana fungicides had made unannounced changes in the fungicides to reduce their toxicity. Not only were shrimp surviving in greater numbers, but also marine life was returning to the Bay of Guayaquil. No one, including Gilberto, understood exactly why—or how—the shrimp industry was reviving. But the reverse in the fortunes of the shrimp industry brought Gilberto a windfall in 1997: he was able to lease his shrimp farm for five years at $800,000 a year!

Gilberto could hardly comprehend the turn of events. When the shrimp industry soured, he did not just take his dwindling fortune and move to Miami for an easier life. He stayed and fought what appeared to be the culprit. It was a lonely fight, though, and with Ecuador's judicial and political system it was—in retrospect—futile. When it became clear that no immediate solution was in sight, Gilberto did the prudent thing and diversified his investments, again bringing on work and risk. But a quirk of nature accomplished what neither science or politics could achieve—the restoration of the shrimp industry. And the same "natural force" wreaked havoc on his alternative investment, which was supposed to shield him from the collapse of the shrimp industry.

If Gilberto was not saddled with the mango plantation, he could live a comfortable life of leisure, thanks to his shrimp farm. What he could do with $800,000 a year! But Gilberto now could not turn his back on the mango plantation, even though it was presently nothing but a sinkhole for money and an administrative headache. Gilberto concluded that the future could bring more surprises. El Niño would not last forever. Maybe the fortunes of the mango and shrimp businesses would again be reversed.

There was, though, no such reversal of fortune. The company that rented his shrimp farm lost money in 1997, in part because of delays in reviving production. With the help of El Niño, 1998 was a profitable year for the company. Still, Gilberto concluded that if he averaged the company's returns for 1997 and 1998, he had come out ahead just leasing the farm. Yet, to everyone's surprise, 1999 and 2000 were devastating years for shrimp production because of diseases. Gilberto was pressured into agreeing to a 50 percent reduction in rent for the year 2000. He increasingly believed that the shrimp business was "all but finished" in Ecuador.

The mango business in Ecuador also looked doomed. In ten years Gilberto had yet to make a profit. The mango farm continued, year after year, to be a sinkhole for money and time. The costs of production and transportation were too high to be able to compete against Mexico, Brazil, and even neighboring Peru. Gilberto increasingly thought of just giving the farm away to someone—anyone.

I remember standing on the bank of a shrimp pool with Gilberto when the shrimp business was at its nadir and the future seemed so gloomy. Gilberto was despondent. He methodically detailed his options. Gilberto did not seem to expect an opinion from me, so I just listened. But as I listened to him I thought of what I would do if I was him. I certainly would not risk $1.5 million in another cycle of shrimp production. I would not experiment with cultivating fish either. What if they died, too? Diversification seemed prudent, but if I had $1.5 million in cash I would not bother cultivating mangoes. The project would surely be a lot of work, and something could go wrong. No, I thought, I would just live off the bonanza of the previous good years cultivating shrimp.

The passage of just a few years suggested that my caution was well placed. But I never would have had the drive or the toleration for risk to enter the shrimp business in the first place. With my character, I would have just stayed at the sugar refinery where Gilberto had worked before daring to be an entrepreneur. All countries, and perhaps especially those that are poorer, need entrepreneurs like Gilberto. But do all countries—and those in Latin America in particular—encourage, nurture, and reward entrepreneurship?

The proliferation of macroeconomic statistics from Latin America, of swings in growth rates, of fluctuations in inflation rates and the like, masks the activities of individuals like Gilberto and, in particular, the struggles they confront to produce goods and services. Of course, no one entrepreneur and his or her activities can be said to be representative of what makes up the "gross national product" of a country or a region. Certainly, most entrepreneurs in Latin America have decidedly fewer resources than Gilberto. For many, capital consists of nothing more than an old Singer sewing machine, a battered pickup truck, or something similar. Still, Gilberto's saga is illustrative.

Despite considerable debate and fits of experimentation with the state as an economic producer, Latin America concluded the twentieth century with an overwhelming commitment to "markets," that is to say leaving economic activity in the hands of private individuals and firms. As Gilberto's personal history shows, there are fortunes to be made. And just as has been the case since the time of European conquest and colonialism, much of the money is still made tapping—directly or indirectly—the natural bounty of the region, be it copper in Chile, plywood in Brazil, soybeans in Argentina, or shrimp in Ecuador. There are, to be sure, "industrial sectors." But if one factors out foreign companies that manufacture in the region—Ford in Mexico, Intel in Costa Rica, Mercedes Benz in Brazil, the myriad of "assembly plants" (*maquiladores*) in the Dominican Republic, and so forth—these industrial sectors are considerably less impressive. There are other sectors where money is made—and lost—most notably construction and "commerce." (These last two sectors fulfill local demand.)

For all kinds of entrepreneurs, in every sector of the economy, there is money to be made in Latin America. But considerable work is needed—and risk entailed—to produce goods and services, even when nature's bounty is being harvested. Entrepreneurs face a web of difficulties: monopolies, inadequate infrastructure, a poorly educated labor force, unwieldy regulations, expensive credit, mediocre service from government institutions (there is a four-year wait for telephones in Nicaragua), corrupt public officials, high rates of theft and other crime, as well as the expected vicissitudes of nature and the world economy.

Efforts to measure national "competitiveness" by the World Bank, the World Economic Forum, or the International Institute for Management Development (a management school in Lausanne, Switzerland) confirm that the "business environment" of most countries in Latin America poses considerable challenges to entrepreneurs. The indexes, though, suggest an exception—Chile. The country not only has a strong commitment to "deregulation" and a commitment to the provision of efficient service on the part of government bureaucracies, but also is noticeably free from corruption. If Latin America remains committed to private economic activity, a central task of governors in the twenty-first century will be to provide a more hospitable environment for entrepreneurs. Economic initiatives will always entail toil and risk, but in most countries of the region the burden can be significantly reduced.

# Chapter 7

## Environmental Degradation

V ENEZUELA'S LAKE Maracaibo is not, in fact, a lake but instead an enormous and ecologically complex estuary. It is composed of four zones: (1) the body of water commonly called Lake Maracaibo, (2) the Maracaibo Estuary, (3) the Bay of El Tablazo, and (4) the Gulf of Venezuela. The first and largest zone, Lake Maracaibo, extends 150 kilometers measured on a north-south axis and, at its widest, 110 kilometers measured on an east-west axis. One hundred thirty-five rivers empty into the "lake," with the largest river being the Catatumbo. The average depth of Lake Maracaibo is 25 meters. There are 112 species of fish in the lake, testament to the biological richness of the estuary.

The Maracaibo Estuary is 40 kilometers long and between 6 and 17 kilometers wide. Its average depth is 10 meters. The Bay of El Tablazo is also huge, with a width of 27 kilometers (measured on an east-west axis) and a length of 24 kilometers (measured on a north-south axis). The Bay of El Tablazo is shallow, with an average depth of only 3 meters, but with 25 percent of its area having a depth of 1.5 meters or less. Beyond the Bay of El Tablazo is the Gulf of Venezuela, linking the entire estuary to the Caribbean—and the world at large.

Lake Maracaibo is renowned for oil. The lake and surrounding area has one of the richest deposits of petroleum in the world. Oil has been extracted from the lake continuously since 1914. Two and a half million barrels of oil are produced daily! Petrochemicals are also produced here. On the east side of the Maracaibo Estuary is the petrochemical complex El Tablazo, one of the ten largest in the world. With all of this oil being extracted and carried off to markets in the United States and elsewhere, and with the production of petrochemicals, too, it is no surprise that Lake Maracaibo has suffered ecological damage. Indeed, there are five thousand active wells in the lake (or the immediate vicinity). And there are another fifteen thousand inactive wells. Moreover, there are somewhere between 20,000 and 40,000 kilometers of oil pipes in the lake, most of which long ago ceased to be used. As one Venezuelan put it, "The bottom of Lake Maracaibo is like a plate of spaghetti." To save costs, everything has always just been left in the lake after its productive use ended. But, unfortunately, something is always breaking, leading to a spill, or snaring something that, in turn, causes a rupture.

The first exploitation of oil in Lake Maracaibo was by North American firms. But in 1975 Venezuela nationalized the petroleum industry, putting everything under the control of a state holding company, Petróleos de Venezuela S.A. (PDVSA). PDVSA is the crown jewel of Venezuela. It is the largest company in Latin America and the generator of enormous wealth for the state—and, by extension, for the country. Oil provides over 90 percent of Venezuela's export income and about two-thirds of its fiscal revenues.

PDVSA is generally held to be a paradigm of efficient administration (at least in comparison with other state oil companies in Latin America). The managers of PDVSA do not compare the company with other companies in Venezuela; they hold themselves to the standards of the major "international" oil companies of the world, firms that are based in the United States or Europe. Emulating the principal oil companies of the United States and Europe has led, among other things, to a heightened sense of environmental responsibility within PDSVA.

Venezuela, moreover, has a ministry charged with protecting the environment. The establishment of such ministries has become fashionable in Latin America, but Venezuela was the first country in the region to establish one, doing so in 1976. The ministry is not viewed as a "powerful" ministry, but it is held to be politically neutral and professional. The ministry's authority was heightened by the passage in 1992 of a package of environmental laws that detailed unacceptable kinds of environmental degradation and imposed harsh penalties—including imprisonment—for violators.

Much can be gleaned about environmental degradation in Venezuela (and, by extension, Latin America at large) by looking carefully at a clash between the El Tablazo petrochemical complex and two neighboring communities. It is illuminating to see what gets defined as an environmental issue (and what does not), who gets blamed (and who does not), and what gets done to resolve a perceived problem and why, in fact, action is taken. The conclusions are sobering.

The El Tablazo complex has eighteen plants, some of them of "mixed" ownership, but most of them belonging to Pequiven, the state petrochemical company that is one of the "holdings" of PDSVA. When the complex, with all of its factories, was constructed, it was perceived locally as positive, above all for the employment it generated. It is now freely conceded that initially the petrochemical complex generated considerable pollution. Even mercury was released into the estuary. Ongoing efforts at modernization have included efforts to curb the generation of solid and atmospheric wastes. But gases are still released, the odors of which can reach the large city (of 1.5 million) of Maracaibo, which lies across the estuary.

A serious challenge to Pequiven, though, came from two neighboring villages, both small: El Hornito, home to three hundred families, and Curva del Pato, home to sixty families. These villages antedated the petrochemical complex. Many men from the villages, however, came to work at the El Tablazo complex. In the early 1980s, under the leadership of a schoolteacher, residents of the two villages began to assert that Pequiven's factories were damaging their health. Skin problems, serious illnesses, and even birth defects were traced to Pequiven's factories. Walls in the villages were adorned with slogans: "Prison and punishment for the delinquents who poison the people and assassinate the environment," "There is no life! I want opportunity," and "Close Pequiven." The local media were contacted; there were reports on the radio and articles in the newspapers. In 1991 a French team made a video about the dispute, giving the villagers ample opportunity to make their claims. The video was not only shown on French television, but parts of it were picked up and shown—very briefly—on Cable News Network (CNN).

Even before the release of the French video, though, Pequiven made a decision to relocate the two communities. In 1990 a census was made of the two communities, and plans were made—with the participation of the villagers—for where and how the communities could be relocated. The first families were moved in 1994–1995. No expense was spared in an effort to please. The new settlements were neatly laid out, with small but sturdy houses. There was running water and electricity in all houses, schools, a church, a fishing center, recreational facilities, and a commitment to plant five thousand trees.

Pequiven did all this, and spent a considerable amount of effort publicizing the resettlement, not because officials were convinced that the communities had been wronged. No, officials thought the claims of illness, birth defects, and the like were unfounded. However, the officials of Pequiven, like officials throughout PDSVA, considered themselves very visible and very vulnerable. True, the environmental degradation of Lake Maracaibo that comes from the petroleum sector is the most visible. But there are many sources of pollution in the area. What is distinct, and what makes PDSVA vulnerable, is the realization that the state enterprise is flush with resources—with cash.

PDSVA officials not only realize that they are viewed as "the goose that lays the golden eggs," but feel very nervous about the potential for local politicians to seize upon any festering problem for their own political ends. As one Stanford University–educated official said, in the luxury of his well-appointed office in Caracas, "We [in the company] are doing well. But Venezuela is not doing well. And with our country's politicians, this combination is very dangerous." So PDSVA paid what many consider an enormous amount of money to relocate the communities of El Hornito and Curva del Pato, not for environmental reasons but to protect itself politically. Likewise, the company generously reimburses fishermen who claim their catch or their equipment has been damaged by oil spills, old pipes, or anything else that seemingly can be blamed on the petroleum industry. Moreover, PDSVA prints lots of promotional material, boasting of its commitment to protect the environment. Indeed, the offices of the ministry charged with protecting the environment are filled with posters from PDSVA.

It is good that PDSVA minds the environment. And it seemingly makes no difference if part of this commitment stems from a nationalist bid to emulate the standards of the "leading" petroleum firms in the world. Through a variety of channels, international norms about the importance of the environment and the responsibility of firms have filtered into Venezuela, especially among the young and the well educated. And it does not matter, either, if PDSVA is especially vigilant about the environment because it fears being smeared by opportunistic politicians who will seize upon any act of negligence. Similar fears exist elsewhere. But the responsiveness of PDSVA is misleading. It is held to high standards, it has the resources to meet those standards, and it can be cajoled into meeting those standards. But the environmental degradation of Lake Maracaibo has many diverse sources. The nonpetroleum sources go largely unnoticed, and—in any case—there is no one in a position to provide redress.

Four major sources of pollution are wreaking havoc with the ecology of Lake Maracaibo. One source is the petroleum industry. Another source is raw sewage: the city of Maracaibo, Venezuela's second largest city, has no sewage treatment plant. None of the other cities on the shores of the lake have sewage treatment plants either. There are "plans" for building treatment plants, but there never has been enough money to bring them to fruition. So sewage just runs out into Lake Maracaibo. Given the warm climate of the area and the slowness with which water in the estuary circulates, this raw sewage poses a serious health threat. But expectations for local government are so low that no one puts pressure on either the city government of Maracaibo or on the authorities at the provincial level. The contrast with expectations for PDVSA is striking.

A third source of pollution to Lake Maracaibo comes from industry. There are 120 industrial plants along the shore, producing everything from packaged dairy products to cement. Most of these plants discharge waste material into the lake. The government does not have the capacity to monitor these firms, though some effort is made. But again, there is no public outcry to halt this source of pollution.

The fourth source of pollution to Lake Maracaibo is held to be, today, the most deadly: it is pollutants swept into the lake from the Catatumbo River, which provides 70 percent of the lake's "fresh" water. The Catatumbo River is 300 kilometers long, with the first 100 kilometers being inside Colombia. Within this stretch there a number of cities, including Pampolona, on the banks of the river. Sewage and waste residues from tanneries and other businesses are just dumped into the river. Once the river enters into Venezuela, it passes through an agricultural zone where pesticides and chemical fertilizers are used. Residues are washed into the river. By the time the waters of the Catatumbo River reach Lake Maracaibo, they are foul. Indeed, it is estimated that 60–70 percent of the pollution of Lake Maracaibo now comes from the Catatumbo River. (The second most consequential source of pollution is generally held to be the raw sewage from the city of Maracaibo and from other, smaller cites.)

At times, the Catatumbo River poses a special threat. Guerrilla groups have blown up sections of an oil pipeline in Colombia, spilling large amounts of oil in the watershed of the Catatumbo River. The total amount of oil that has been "spilled" is said to exceed the amount of oil spilled off the coast of Alaska by the tanker *Exxon Valdez*. The Colombian state oil company, Ecopetrol, is given high marks for its ability to contain the damage, but inevitably the Catatumbo River is contaminated.

There is no thought as to how the Catatumbo River can be safeguarded from these varied sources of pollution. There are so many sources of pollution, some of which originate in another country, and there is no one who can be readily made to assume responsibility. So next to nothing is said about these sources of damage to the ecology of Lake Maracaibo.

A pattern emerges in Venezuela of identifying environmental degradation with concentrated, visible acts, by a perpetrator who is identifiable and who, it can be conceived, might either avoid doing the damage altogether or, being flush enough with resources, be forced into retribution. There is logic to thinking in this fashion, but it is a facile logic, grounded in political and administrative expediency. An examination of Lake Maracaibo, though, suggests environmental degradation is not only an important issue, but also one that is complex. There are many sources of pollution and many perpetrators. The most visible kinds—or sources—of environmental degradation are not necessarily the most pernicious. Likewise, not all perpetrators are easily identifiable or able to be forced into changing their behavior.

The most discussed environmental issue in Latin America is the destruction of the region's forests. Some of the world's highest deforestation rates are in Latin America. There is concern about what is left of Mexico's forests, of the tropical forests of Central America, but most attention is focused on the Amazon, which is the largest single geographical feature of the South American continent. It is both a river and a giant river valley. What is referred to as the Amazon jungle is the tropical rain forest covering an area drained by the Amazon River and its hundreds of tributaries. Together, river and forest form Amazonia, what the world calls the Amazon. The jungle is estimated to cover an area the size of Western Europe (or the United States west of the Mississippi River). It includes parts of eight countries: Brazil, Peru, Colombia, Ecuador, Bolivia, Venezuela, Suriname, and Guyana. The largest portions are in Brazil and Peru, where, in both countries, the Amazon makes up about half the land area. If it were a country, the Amazon would be the ninth largest in the world.

The Amazon River draws its initial strength from hundreds of small streams in the Andes Mountains, tumbling through steep gorges and eventually forming a kilometer-and-a-half-wide flow in northern Peru, which grows to more than five kilometers for parts of its length in Brazil. As it crosses the Peruvian border, the Amazon runs into an enormous shallow bowl that makes up most of the center of South America. It is a remarkably flat basin that, if it were stripped of trees, might look like the Great Plains of the United States or the Sahara of Africa. Through the middle of the bowl, the Amazon River cuts a deep trough that drops only thirty meters in its final 2,500-kilometer course to the Atlantic Ocean. The river's immense power comes from the many large tributaries that force their way into the channel.

Possibly because of the Andes's effect on the formation of rain clouds, the Amazon is—at least presently—one of the wettest places in the world. There are variations in rainfall among different parts of the basin and during different seasons, but the climate is quite stable. The combination of a wet and stable climate has produced an immense variety of plant life. The vegetation that covers the basin is held to represent, roughly, one-half of the remaining forest on earth. Moreover, the basin is, in variety of living things, the richest area of the earth. Perhaps 1 million of the world's estimated 5 million species of plants and animals live in the Amazon. Many of these species have yet to be studied for their potential medicinal, nutritional, or ecological values. Finally, the Amazon has 20 percent of the world's freshwater supply.

It is the Amazon that gives Latin America its principal forests. In 2000, the percentage of land in forest per country was as follows: Brazil, 66 percent; Peru, 53 percent; Colombia, 52 percent; Venezuela, 52 percent; Bolivia, 45 percent; Ecuador, 43 percent. But in each of these countries the forest is under assault. There is logging, but by most accounts the majority of trees are just burned to clear land for agriculture or simply so that ownership can be claimed. Indeed, it is suggested that since 1950 the most important change in land use in tropical Latin America has been the widespread conversion of forest to pasture. But, again, while the livestock—cattle—are an important economic activity, generating wealth, cattle have also been attractive because they have low labor and supervision requirements, present limited risk, but can be employed to "stake a claim" of land ownership and use.

As the review of environmental degradation of Lake Maracaibo suggests, there are many sources—or kinds—of assaults to the Amazon and its forests. Although the Amazon itself remains sparsely populated, population growth elsewhere—on the borders—generates pressure for extending the "agricultural frontier" and for tapping the many resources of the region. Latin America's population in 1950 was 163 million inhabitants. In 2000 the population was estimated to be 458 million. The Amazon, like the forests in southern Mexico, the Petén in Guatemala, the Atlantic Coast in Nicaragua, and so forth, is a "safety valve." The poor, the landless, the dispossessed encroach upon the forests. But desires for national "security," for "development," and sheer greed also endanger the Amazon and the other forests of the region.

For example, the military governments of Brazil (of 1930 to 1945 and from 1964 to 1989) viewed the country's vast forest, sparsely populated and bordered by seven countries, as a security threat. In the late 1960s the military government enacted a series of legislation, as part of "Operation Amazonia," committing the state to the occupation and development of the region. There were tax credit subsidies for investment, income tax exemptions and deductions, and subsidized credit for encouraging "development" in the Amazon. Furthermore, land titles were secured by "improving" the land, which was interpreted as clearing it of forests. Titles provided ownership to an area that was a multiple of the tract that had been cleared, thus providing incentives to deforest—through burning—large areas. This "development" was further stimulated by an ambitious road-building campaign.

While the Brazilian military ceded power to a civilian government in the 1980s, it maintains a strong presence in the north of Brazil and continues to stress the strategic importance of developing the Amazon. Many of the more generous subsidies and tax breaks were eliminated in 1989, but others remain. Brazil's democracy has been unable either to halt the anarchical destruction of the Amazon's forests or to devise and implement a sustainable strategy for the exploitation of the forests. In fact, successive democratic governments have undertaken major infrastructure projects that span large expanses of the basin—intended to accelerate the development of the timber, agriculture, mining, and industrial sectors of the sprawling economy. The cumulative effects of these massive projects—and the expansion of road networks—on the Amazon have not been assessed systematically. There is no "plan." Nascent efforts to promote conservation—and planning—in the Amazon are overwhelmed by diverse pressures that lead, in turn, to destructive trends.

As in Lake Maracaibo, throughout the Amazon there are many sources of environmental degradation. Moreover, the public is either disinterested or has a narrow view of what constitutes environmental degradation, and of what kind of actor can be held responsible. The state has conflictive incentives with regard to the stewardship of the environment, and—in any case—even well-informed and virtuous governors do not have sufficient authority to resolve what is, in fact, a most complex issue.

The contamination of water, deforestation, pollution of the atmosphere, disposing of waste—these and similar issues rose to prominence at the end of the twentieth century. These environmental problems, however, have not been resolved; indeed, the extent of their import has scarcely begun to be realized. The problems have been bequeathed to the governors of the twenty-first century. A question, though, suggests itself. Does liberalism give Latin Americans the ability to tackle successfully environmental degradation? The evidence to date is not promising, which is worrisome, especially since certain kinds of damage are irreversible.

# Chapter 8

## Malls

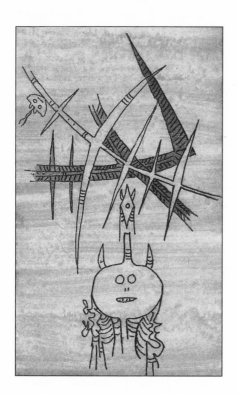

THE ZIMBABWEAN novelist Chenjerai Hove has said, "In hard times the artist will blend images of despair with those of hope. In good times the writer will depict the madness of over-eating at the expense of cultivating other values." In Latin America today these are "good times"— economies are on the rebound, prosperity is welcome, and it is hard to question the free trade strategy that has led to growth. However, the spending frenzy of those with wealth and income invokes Chenjerai's image of "the madness of over-eating."

A Harvard-trained professor of marketing who works throughout the region asserts, "The desire in Latin America today is for satisfaction and as soon as possible." And satisfaction, apparently, is shopping. Indeed, "shopping" is one of the most commonly used English words throughout the hemisphere (as in, *Ay, lo que me gusta es ir de* shopping *a Miami*). Nothing captures the prevailing mood in Latin America so well as the explosion of malls throughout the region. If the 1980s in Latin America was the "lost decade," because of a continentwide recession that led to an average per capita fall in income of 25 percent, the 1990s in Latin America was the "mall decade." The twentieth century in Latin America ended—for those with money—with a shopping spree. This "acquisitiveness" is a legacy for the twenty-first century.

On any Saturday afternoon, Bogotá's grand Plaza de Bolívar is all but deserted. The crowd is at the Unicentro Mall, with its 360 stores. Surrounding it is the competition, more malls: Metrópolis, Granahorrar, Andino, Hacienda Santa Barbara, Centro 93, Plaza de las Américas, and so forth. Signs announce the construction of even more malls and their coming attractions: excellent street access, elevators with panoramic views, fast-food patios, ample parking, 117 stores. At these malls Colombians can shop in stores with names like Jeans & Jackets. For lunch there are the likes of fast-food restaurant Kokoriko, which offers "Kokori-nuggets" (pieces of deep-fried chicken) served on Styrofoam plates. Judging from the late-model cars in the parking lots, the display of fine clothes, jewelry, and cellular phones, Colombians in the malls spend and spend.

While shopping, they are likely to discuss Bogotá's traffic. Studies show that, on average, it takes ninety minutes to go from house to office in the morning, and another ninety minutes in the afternoon to go from office to house. The origin of the problem is in "success": with a strong economy and lower tariffs (part of the commercial opening), the number of cars in Bogotá doubled in just four years. And car imports continue apace.

But not just cars are easier to buy. The new economic development strategy facilitates the appearance at the Carulla supermarket of such imports from the United States as Nach-Olé Tortilla Chips, Betty

Crocker Super Moist Fudge Marble Cake Mix, and Pedigree Puppy Dog Food. The store detective who keeps an eye on the aisles against shoplifting wears a bulletproof vest, testament not only to the violence in Colombia, but also a stark reminder that the poor majority in Colombia cannot afford these foreign temptations.

In Costa Rica the story is the same. San José's Plaza de la Cultura is now bordered by McDonald's, Archie's, Burger King, and Taco Bell. If one is not eating out, the fashionable place to shop for groceries is the Japanese supermarket, Yaohan. With Costa Rica, too, embracing free trade, shoppers can now buy—in a country that exports mangoes—canned mango juice from Taiwan and Israel. If you just want water, there is a choice among French, Italian, and Canadian bottled water. There is potting soil imported from Germany. And there is lots of imported pet food; Costa Rican pet food is now a $6 million market. Even "kitty litter" is imported.

In the early 1990s, the number of cars in Costa Rica increased by 40 percent. Japanese cars are the most popular, but there are new Volvos, BMWs, and Mercedes-Benzes. The places to go in these cars are the malls, such as Multi Plaza, with some 200 stores, or the newer, hit-of-the-town, Mall San Pedro. The outside construction of the Mall San Pedro is described locally as "fake Flintstone rocks," but inside are Victoria's Secret and 259 other temptations. On one Sunday there were an estimated sixty thousand visitors to the mall, described in the press as "a shopper's delight." There are many smaller *centros de comercio* in Costa Rica, too, one of which does not allow entrance if you do not arrive in a car (the smart way to keep out those who have no money).

Malls are going up elsewhere in Latin America, from Buenos Aires to Tijuana. In Quito there are now eight malls, the largest of which has about 400 stores. Aside from clothing, hardly anything for sale in the mall is made in Ecuador. Even in impoverished Nicaragua, where unemployment is rampant, those few with money are in a consumer frenzy, especially for imported goods. Despite a decade of revolutionary rule, success in Managua is today measured by what you drive, with the apex being a large Toyota Land Cruiser. La Colonia supermarket at the Plaza de España offers frozen brussels sprouts, Bugles Corn Snacks, Kraft Miniature Marshmallows, and—in a country whose principal export is coffee—Maxwell House Coffee. Managua has two malls: the Inter-Plaza and the Metro-Centro.

El Salvador's civil war in the 1980s led to a massive flight of Salvadorans to the United States. Many have returned, at least to visit their families. Maybe these *hermanos lejanos* (distant brothers and sisters) have brought back the "consumer tastes" of the United States. The popular mall, Galerías, in San Salvador includes the following stores: Home

Gallery, Park Ave Shoes, Sandy's Hallmark Shop, Mike Mike, Radio Shack, Mothertime, The Original Levi's Store, and The Book Shop (which sells the *National Enquirer*). Some of the stores have signs in their windows announcing, "Big Sales." There is a food court at the mall, featuring Biggest, Mister Donut, Cajun Grill, Subway, and Quick Sandwich. The novelty of the mall is that you can combine shopping and prayer; inserted among the stores is the Capilla San José, which posts hours for mass. At another of the city's malls, the Plaza Merlot, there is a grim reminder of the country's continuing violence, now over-whelmingly criminal: a sign at the entrance of the supermarket Super Selecto states, "Please check your gun at the door."

Mexico City has its shopping malls, among them Pabellón Al-tavista, Centro Coyoacán, Centro Histórico, Centro Santa Fe, Galerías Coapa, Perisur, and Plaza Satélite. One celebrated department store (El Palacio de Hierro) announces sales with the copy, "Women on the Verge of a Shopping Attack" (sometimes accompanied by a picture of a sun-glasses-wearing woman with her mouth wide open). Given Mexico City's pollution and crime, it is not surprising, perhaps, that there are offers for Venta-Airwashers (Europe's number one specialist for air pu-rifiers and humidifiers) and for the BMW Security Concept: "security cars," "armored automobiles," "equipment and security systems," and "drivers training programs." The state of Texas places ads in Mexico City's newspapers announcing, "There is more to do in Texas than go shopping." Underneath the caption it is explained that there are, in fact, many shopping malls, that they are very large, and that they are in all parts of the state. But there are so many things to do in Texas: "*un día en todo Texas es mucho más que todo un día en el* mall." The copy closes by asking, in a not very convincing fashion, "Of course you can always come shopping, but wouldn't you rather spend a hot day float-ing down a river in an inner tube?"

But perhaps it is Tijuana that most forcefully demonstrates the ex-cesses and cultural confusion of Latin America's consumer binge. Ti-juana's border with San Diego is said to be the most heavily crossed border in the world. The center of Tijuana is still Revolution Boulevard ("Revu" as it is called by young *rockeros*), just as it was during prohibi-tion, when the city began luring tourists from San Diego and Los An-geles. There are still bars in Tijuana, but more than anything else there are shops offering a profusion of cheap trinkets (and piñatas of Winnie the Pooh) to tourists who do not seem to either expect or want anything else. More refined, or at least cleaner and more wholesome, are the shopping centers where Tijuana's middle class shops.

The Plaza Río Tijuana is one such mall. The high-end department store, Dorian's, sells cosmetics and perfume from Ralph Lauren, Helena

Rubinstein, Lancôme, and the like. More lowbrow is the huge Comercial Mexicana (with a bank of twenty-nine cash registers between the entrance and the exit). There are cosmetics here, too, but mostly there are goods for the "family": Evian water, Kool-Aid, Whirlpool refrigerators, and—in the front of the store—lots of toys for the children. Prominently displayed is the twenty-one-piece set called "Hercules Gunship, Made in the U.S.A.: AC-130 Gunship (with 3 pivoting machine guns), 19 plastic soldiers, American flag with stand, and a sheet of colorful labels." There are also big boxes of the "Pink Fashion Girl Stretch Limousine (Hot Tub Holds Four Dolls!), 32 inches long, Made in the U.S.A." After sorting through all the choices, a break can be taken at the Restaurant McArthur (it offers hamburgers).

The truly rich of Latin America are likely to forgo local malls and to shop in the United States and Europe. Brazil, enormous and inequitable, has gotten noticed as a country that sends big spenders to New York. An article in the *New York Times* in the spring of 1998 (April 5) was titled "Foreigners Buy up New York":

> The sales staff at the Chanel Boutique on East 57th Street can speak 24 languages. . . . One of the most crucial languages to know is Portuguese. Store managers indicate that over the last few years Brazilians have merged as the most avid shoppers. That impression is backed up by statistics from the new York Convention and Visitors Bureau, which reports that in 1995, the most recent year for which figures are available, Brazilian visitors allotted 36 percent of their average daily expenditures to shopping—$96 a day out of an average $267, which was also the second-highest average daily expenditure of the 10 countries included. . . . And given that Brazilians spent more time in the city, their collective shopping spree totaled even more [than that of visitors from other countries].

Similarly, Brazilians have become conspicuous in the upscale ski resorts of Vail, Colorado, where package tours for Brazilians often include trips to Denver's largest malls.

Brazilians can shop in their own malls, too. The newly moneyed in Rio de Janeiro abound in the Barra da Tijuca, the fastest-growing neighborhood of the city. Here there is an entertainment mall called the New York City Center, as well as malls named Barra Shopping, Barra Garden, Barra Point, and Barra Square. In these malls are stores—some advertising "sales" instead of the equivalent Portuguese word—with such captivating names as World Top Lock, Bike Box, Bad Kid, and Water Planet.

For some wealthy Latin Americans, the exalted place to shop is not the local mall, not a mall in Houston or Miami, or even the emporiums of Madison Avenue in New York, but instead the boutiques of Milan. Still, what remains impressive is the extent to which malls have become a fixture in Latin America, the degree to which they have captured the interest of so many Latin Americans, and the myriad of imported products—and cultural practices—they offer.

Latin America's malls are clearly a United States import. The world's first fully enclosed indoor shopping center was built in Minnesota in 1956 (a year after the opening of Disneyland). Between 1970 and 1990, twenty-five thousand new shopping centers were opened in the United States, one every seven hours. One of the few studies of the phenomenon is a brief book titled *The Mall: An Attempted Escape from Everyday Life*. The work, written by Jerry Jacobs, a sociologist, asserts that malls are attractive precisely because "nothing unusual is happening." Perhaps malls are appealing in Latin America because they offer an escape from the hard edges of urban life: congestion, crime, and an intrusive poverty.

But the fashion for malls is also inextricably tied to the commercial opening in Latin America. People would not flock to malls to gawk at— and purchase—locally produced consumer goods. An earlier "development strategy" featured "import substitution," which prescribed high tariffs to protect—and encourage—locally produced goods. The hope was to produce a wide range of goods and services, not just a handful of tropical commodities for export. The intellectual fashion now is for "free trade" and "export promotion": a level playing field is all that is judged necessary to ensure economic development. Entrepreneurs will find and exploit comparative advantages within each nation. At least to date, in most countries this strategy has not resulted in much more than the addition of new tropical export commodities to the familiar list of coffee, bananas, and sugar (as well as oil and minerals). Now there are also exports of grapes, mangoes, ferns and flowers, macadamia nuts, asparagus, and the like, plus a few finished goods such as doors, as well as the output of factories established by multinationals taking advantage of cheap labor.

This strategy of development does not look so terribly different from nineteenth-century laissez-faire. So far, though, the macroeconomic statistics of export earnings and of the growth of the gross national product are encouraging. Maybe the strategy, coupled with more prudent government fiscal and monetary policies, will usher in sustainable economic growth. But the consumer frenzy accompanying the region's economic growth is disturbing. Economists worry that the propensity to import is too high and that it will overwhelm export earnings, leading to familiar pressures on the exchange rate. The December 1994 collapse of the Mexican peso and the pressure on the Brazilian real and Ecuador's sucre in 1999 show how vulnerable Latin American countries remain to collapsing exchange rates. (Economists also worry that too much of recent economic growth has been driven by unsustainable capital inflows.)

But the consumer frenzy is a worry for more than economists. Now that the region has bit of breathing space, elites are not taking a hard look at deep structural problems and trying to identify solutions. Poverty is ignored, as are so many other problems, including the need to consolidate incipient democracies. The paralyzing ideological wars are over, the deep recession of the 1980s has ended, and—to generalize grossly—those fortunate few who decide everything are at the mall shopping. Moreover, the enjoyment of malls—and the pride in local malls—suggests many have been persuaded to believe that "how you shop is who you are," that shopping is a statement about your place in society, and maybe even your part—or place—in the world's "culture."

The beginning of a new century in Latin America does not show signs of being an era of intellectual or political fervor. To be sure, there are congressional debates, corruption scandals, and election campaigns. But it is hard to identify journals and books, let alone social movements and political parties, that discuss with passion and creativity the problems of individual countries or of the region at large. Bookstores throughout the region offer noticeably fewer books on politics than in previous decades. Taking their place are shelves of "self-help" books and translations of the best-sellers of United States business schools. For example, the bookstore of the Universidad Centroamericana "José Simeon Cañas" in San Salvador, a university once thoroughly politicized, now offers Bill Gates, *Camino al futuro*, and a score of books that bear stickers saying "Bestseller de *Business Week*." Other than literary works, there are few books on El Salvador or Latin America at large. The only whiff of dissent comes from odd volumes with titles like *Guía popular para la práctica de la agricultura orgánica*.

Likewise, many previous centers of political activity are dormant. A dean at the Catholic University of Ecuador revealed much when he said, in the privacy of his office, that Ecuador's universities today play only a reactionary role, that they have no ideas of their own to put forward, that they only attempt to put a brake, faintly, on changes instituted by others. Students at Chile's renowned universities, held to be the best in the region, are quiet, taken up with concerns about their budding careers. Status is not pursuing research in the social sciences (or humanities), but instead being in a fast-track Master of Business Administration (MBA) program, perhaps at the newly minted, but already prestigious, Adolfo Ibañez University.

The "left" in Latin America committed many sins: reckless use of violence, promotion of economic follies, factionalism, and more. But it kept the issue of poverty on everyone's mind, and it held out a dream of a more egalitarian society, where basic needs were met. Maybe it even served as a check on the most blatant displays of consumerism. It was noisy and persistent. But now the left has all but vanished, having been swallowed by electoral politics, consumerism, and nihilism. The social Christian political parties have in the past committed themselves to many of the same ends (via different means), but they seem now to have strayed from their mission. Today they, too, are "at the mall." There is no one "stirring things up," asking hard questions about state and society, and offering a vision of how Latin America should evolve as a new century dawns.

Will a new generation of activists emerge? If so, where will they come from and what will be their vision? The trenchant problems of Latin America, where nearly a quarter of the population continues to live in what is defined by the World Bank as "extreme poverty," ensure that the region is not at the end of politics, but at some uncertain beginning. Malls may become a fixture of Latin America, but they are unlikely to hold everyone's attention forever. Indeed, in 1980 the per capita number of hours per month spent in the United States in malls was 7.5; by 1994 the number of hours had fallen to 1.4.

# Chapter 9

## Crime

THE TELEPHONE rang; Danilo said, "Hello."

"This is Bam-Bam. I hear you have lost something."

"Yes, my car was stolen."

"If you authorize me, *if you authorize me*, I will look for it, providing that you pay me a reward of $2,500 if I am successful in finding it."

Danilo agreed. Three days later Bam-Bam called and told him that his car had been found and that Danilo should bring $2,500 in cash to a specified location. Danilo had two friends, Noel and John, who had their stolen cars recovered after paying a "ransom." But he was still surprised by Bam-Bam's audacity when they met:

"Before you pay me, let us inspect the car to make sure there is no damage."

There was no damage; Danilo handed over the cash.

"Before you go, let me give you some tips on how to protect your car against future theft, although I personally guarantee that your car will not be stolen in the next six months." Prominent among his tips was the installation of an alarm, which Bam-Bam said could be done at a local shop where, he concluded, "Tell them Bam-Bam sent you and you will get a 30 percent discount."

It was true; Danilo got a 30 percent discount.

Bam-Bam, the self-anointed nickname for a handsome young man with a ponytail, was finally arrested in Costa Rica and given a modest prison sentence. But his "business" seemingly soured only because he became such a celebrated figure, to the point of being asked for his autograph on the streets of San José, that the authorities had to act.

Even Danilo could find some amusement in his costly encounter with Bam-Bam. But other "kidnappings" in Latin America are not so benign. Stefano drove up to the still-charming Mexican city of Taxco with a friend in a Volkswagen beetle. Gunmen abducted Stefano, took him to a nearby mountain, and chained him to a tree, keeping a machine gun jammed into his throat and feeding him cans of tuna fish. His family was asked to pay $2 million for his release. The family asked for a more manageable ransom. The kidnappers made Stefano drink a large quantity of pure alcohol and then sliced off a part of his left ear, which they sent to the family. A telephone call followed with a dire threat: next would be a finger, then a hand, and so forth until Stefano was cut into many pieces. Stefano's father, Alberto, contacted the authorities. The governor of the state (Guerrero) paid a visit of consolation, but the police were of no help, proving unable even to tap the phone line. A ransom was finally agreed upon, and Alberto divided the money (nearly all borrowed), as he was instructed, into two piles, half the sum in pesos and the other half in dollars. Twenty-two days after being abducted, Stefano was released, an emotional wreck.

Stefano's saga is far from an isolated case. In 1997 there were, according to the governor, over a hundred *reported* kidnappings in the state of Guerrero. Other states and the Federal District, home of Mexico City, also report a surge in kidnappings and other violent crimes. Indeed, Mexico City is now held to be the third most dangerous city in the world. The wave of kidnappings is notable because this crime is all but nonexistent in most wealthy countries, where good police work makes it all but impossible to avoid capture. Kidnappings, whether of late-model Toyotas or children, are part of contemporary Latin America at least in part because of the absence of competent police.

In many countries of Latin America, from Mexico to Argentina, there is, in fact, the suspicion that the police collaborate or even participate in such violent crimes as kidnappings, as well as more prosaic robberies. Shortly after Stefano's release, the chief of police of the neighboring state of Morelos and two of his aides were arrested as they prepared to dump a cadaver along a road in Guerrero. The tortured body was of a seventeen-year-old member of a kidnapping gang. Mexico's attorney general's office opened an investigation into the Morelos police, declaring that, "it appears these individuals are involved in the protection of gangs dedicated to kidnapping and to narcotics trafficking." Guerrero is likely no different; the police there were just taking offense at their state being used as a "body dump."

The World Bank collects and publishes statistics on violent crime throughout the world. While data on crime is often problematic, figures published by the World Bank confirm anecdotal evidence that crime is a serious—and growing—problem in Latin America. Indeed, according to the World Bank, Latin America as a region suffers from the highest rates of crime in the world. The United States itself has a high rate of crime, including of murder. But Colombia's murder rate is nine times as high. Guatemala and El Salvador's rates are fourteen times as high. In ten of the thirteen countries in Latin America that keep credible records, crime has increased substantially in the last ten to fifteen years. In many countries, crime is growing at an alarming rate. For example, in Panama and Peru homicides have multiplied by a factor of between four and six in just the last ten to fifteen years. And countries such as Honduras and Ecuador, which previously were largely spared such crimes as kidnappings and extortion, now confront them as common occurrences.

A study funded by the World Bank, titled "Institutional Obstacles for Doing Business," surveyed 3,600 entrepreneurs in sixty-nine countries. Latin American respondents had the highest rate of concern about theft and other kinds of crime. Ninety percent of respondents stated that crime is a serious problem. Moreover, 80 percent of respondents in Latin America reported that they did not feel confident that the state authorities protected them and their property from criminals. It was reported, too, that personal safety and the security of property had decreased over the last decade. When presented with a long list of potential obstacles to their activities, business leaders in Latin America reported that their gravest problems are: (1) corruption, (2) inadequate infrastructure, and (3) theft and other crimes. If one defines corruption as nothing more than "theft and other crimes" by public officials, then the dimensions of the problem are truly staggering. Correspondingly, those interviewed in Latin America expressed little confidence in their respective country's judiciary system.

Crime in Latin America is widespread, a plague on all classes, including the poor. In Brazil kidnapping may be as simple as grabbing victims on the street and holding them only briefly, just long enough to empty cash from their bank's automated teller machine. In the slums of Caracas, Venezuela, there are armed robberies of shoes worn by pedestrians, with those balking murdered. (The murder rate in Caracas has increased fivefold in ten years.) In my rural neighborhood of Dulce Nombre in Costa Rica, even the local church was burglarized; the priest's microphone and vestments were stolen (the neighborhood reaction: "the thieves will pass directly to hell").

As elsewhere, Peru has suffered from a rash of crime. In the capital, in Lima, Peruvians have returned home from a day of work to find their home not just "burglarized," but completely emptied—pillows, blankets, sheets, mattresses, and everything else gone. Most disturbing, though, the country's famed colonial churches are being sacked. Precious paintings and artifacts (including crosses), some dating to the sixteenth century, are stolen. In 1999 church officials were estimating that one in ten Peruvian churches had been recently looted.

Crime has become so common in Latin America that it has become a staple of conversations, with the telling of stories and—even—jokes. A Costa Rican colleague recounts how an elderly aunt was startled by the sound of someone breaking into her home. Thinking quickly, she yelled to her maid, "Rosa bring me the pistol." Rosa yelled back, "What pistol? We don't have one." Although elements of humor can be found in the wave of crime plaguing the region, Latin Americans are troubled by the trend.

How can Latin America's surge in crime be explained? Didn't the 1980s and early 1990s bring an end to thirty years of ideological conflict, of militarism, of civil wars, and of authoritarianism? Hasn't there been an embrace of democracy and economic reform in Latin America? Isn't the region supposed to be off to a good start, finally, on the right road? It is understandable, surely, that there is still poverty, difficult to eradicate even with the best of economic models and with high rates of economic growth. But why is there such a dramatic increase in crime throughout the region, in countries as different from one another as Mexico, Costa Rica, Peru, and Argentina? Are there parallels with Russia and South Africa, two countries that have also recently made sweeping political and economic transitions and that, also, suffer from a surge in crime, much of it violent?

Ann Bernstein, a South African long involved in the struggle against apartheid and now director of the Center for Development and Enterprise (in Johannesburg), said in a recent conversation that the two most important issues in South Africa are unemployment and crime. She has a number of explanations for why crime has dramatically increased in South Africa: (1) apartheid created criminals and fostered crime; (2) the movement away from authoritarian rule left weak institutions to fight crime, a poorly trained and ill-paid police force, and judicial and penal systems sorely in need of reform; (3) democracy, with its attendant "liberalization," creates an "opening" for all sorts of activities, including, unfortunately, crime.

Her explanations for why South Africa has suffered a wave of crime is suggestive for Latin America. Guerrilla movements, civil wars, and military governments all led to violence. Some guerrillas and some members of the "security apparatus" have continued to do the only thing they know how to do—use a gun. The rule of law was weak in the region's military governments, and those regimes have bequeathed to today's democracies antiquated laws, poorly trained police forces, and weak judiciary systems. Perhaps, too, the greater freedoms afforded by democracy, and the attendant constraints on coercion, have been exploited by those tempted by the quick gains of crime.

This set of explanations is intuitively plausible. But how does one explain why even those countries in the region with a history of democracy, namely Costa Rica, Colombia, and Venezuela (and perhaps, too, the Dominican Republic), are also experiencing a surge in crime? Alternative explanations are offered. Perhaps fault lies with the "neoliberal" economic model, which has curbed the role of the state and increased, in turn, the role of markets. Despite the gain of greater macroeconomic stability, especially in the control of inflation, there have been costs: battered social programs, rising unemployment, heightened income inequality, and the championing of a crass materialism. So, the reasoning goes, if you can't get wealthy through privatization of state assets or through buying shares in a shopping mall, you will be tempted to rob someone.

Others argue that what is decisive about the neoliberal model is not its economic import, but the extent to which "state capacity" has been undermined, or at least neglected. While it may be advisable to scale back the state's role in the economy, that should not be taken to mean—as it frequently has—that a weak state is desirable. What is needed is a "lean but strong" state, capable of fulfilling the traditional responsibilities of government, including prominently the provision of public order.

A different explanation for the surge in crime is based on culture: the collapse of the family, dislocations from mass migration and rapid population growth, the lack of civic education, the secularization of society, and, among other similarly diffuse forces, the spread of anticivic norms from the United States, with it "gansta rap," gangs, drug culture, and rampant consumerism. It seems facile to draw such parallels as the one between the introduction of music television videos (MTV) and rising crime. But there are ingrained norms and practices in many parts of Latin America that do work against the rule of law and that may provide an amoral staging ground for crime. In Argentina it is joked that the national sport is tax evasion. In Brazil there is an expression, "For my friends, everything; for my enemies, the law!" In Ecuador there is a saying, "The law is for the poncho" (i.e., the poor Indians who wear them). A common quip throughout Latin America is, "*Hecho la ley; hecho el engaño*" (Once a law is made, so is made the loophole).

Corruption in many public institutions, ministries, agencies, even police forces, is endemic. For example, a study conducted in 1996 by Mexico's Secretariat of Administrative Development and Oversight, based on anonymous interviews with police and on payroll information, indicated that police who earn less than $350 a month spend four times their wages. The majority of rank-and-file police interviewed said that if they did not rob common citizens and steal from—as well as collaborate with—criminals, they would be unable to support their families. Those interviewed added that they were not overly concerned with the image they projected; their priority was money. Perhaps even more frightening, in 2000 the government of Argentina purged its "prison service," removing top officers, after allegations that guards had let inmates out for robbing excursions in exchange for "kickbacks." For crime—including corruption—to be reduced in Mexico, in Argentina, and elsewhere in Latin America, it will be necessary, among other tasks, to change attitudes and values; not in everyone—that would be impossible—but large swaths of society need to be persuaded of the importance of the rule of law. And the state—and its representatives—need to be trusted.

The celebrated cartoonist "Quino," from Argentina, has a cartoon showing a somber crowd awaiting the undraping of a statue in a public park. Once the statue is presented, the crowd is beside itself with laughter. The base of the statue (of some dour politician) reads, "He gave everything to his country." A joke tells of two bureaucrats, public servants, one from Mexico and one from Venezuela. The two sometimes meet to work on some ill-defined project. After a meeting in Mexico City, the Mexican asks the Venezuelan if he would like to "come see my house." "Yes." Off they go, in a luxurious car, climbing a mountain, where at the top the Mexican has a gorgeous home. "But," asks the Venezuelan, "how do you have all of this working for the government?" The Mexican says, "Look down there in the valley. See that highway?" "Yes." "Ten percent," says the Mexican. "Ah," says the Venezuelan. The following year the Mexican travels to Venezuela. After their work, the Venezuelan invites the Mexican to his house. Off they go in a helicopter. At the top of a mountain the Venezuelan has a palace. The confused Mexican says, "I thought I lived well. How do you have so much when you work for the government?" The Venezuelan says, "Look down there in the valley. See the dam over the river?" "No, I don't see anything." "One hundred percent."

What is to be done? Before assuming office as mayor of Mexico City, Cuauhtémoc Cárdenas of the center-left Democratic Revolutionary Party (PRD) announced that security would be his top priority. Success eluded Cárdenas—he left office without having reversed the tide of crime. But Cárdenas is one of the few prominent politicians in the region to recognize publicly the importance of crime. The pernicious effect of crime on economic development seems ignored, and so does the extent to which democracy's legitimacy depends on its ability to resolve problems. Greater attention to crime is needed in the region by public officials; they need to think hard about how the surge in crime can be reversed.

It would be easier to proceed if it could be established just why crime has risen so dramatically since the 1980s/1990s in Latin America. But there are many competing explanations, with no way to prove their relative merits. And, in any case, the prominent theories suggest Herculean projects: ending poverty or providing loving families for all. The only viable short-run policy seems to be effective law enforcement. Citizens do not engage in crime for two reasons: (1) the coercive power of the state and (2) the moral authority of the state. The first has been weakened in Latin America by the transition from authoritarianism to democracy, and the second has yet to be established by the new democracies. Building the moral authority of the state is an ambitious and long-term endeavor. So the burden for now seemingly falls on strengthening the coercive power of the state.

Given the sorry state of many of the region's police forces and judicial systems, though, this task cannot be accomplished just by adding to the ranks of the police or by augmenting their ranks with personnel from the armed forces, as has been tried in Mexico and Brazil. Police forces have to be completely rebuilt, and judicial systems need overhauling. There is much to be done.

# Chapter 10

## The Poor

Every year the Inter-American Development Bank publishes a monograph titled *Economic and Social Progress in Latin America*. Most years the reports address a particular topic. Reading the studies can be tedious; they are written by economists who favor a matter-of-fact style. Numbers and charts abound. But the reports invariably contain a wealth of information. Especially compelling is the 1998–1999 report, a monumental study of inequality in Latin America. The report is compelling in part because it is an unparalleled measurement of inequality throughout the region, entailing a staggering amount of work. But the report is also meritorious because it addresses important issues that have been overshadowed by a flurry of attention to the region's financial markets: the stability of currencies, the interest rates set by central banks, the movement of capital, debt repayment schedules, and, above all, the rise and fall of incipient stock markets. Latin America is an "emerging market."

For the overwhelming majority of Latin Americans, though, pressing "economic issues" are immediate and family-centered. Who works, where, and with what remuneration? Income distribution has a direct bearing on these questions, especially since the Inter-American Development Bank study concludes that, on average, the countries of Latin America suffer from the greatest income inequality in the world. The largest and most populous country in Latin America—Brazil—has one of the widest income gaps in the world: the wealthiest 10 percent of the population amass almost 50 percent of national income, while the poorest 50 percent of the population scrape together little more than 10 percent.

Besides Brazil, the most inequitable countries in Latin America are Chile, Guatemala, Ecuador, Mexico, Panama, and Paraguay. By regional standards, Costa Rica and Uruguay have less inequity. For the region at large: the wealthiest 5 percent of the population receive 25 percent of national income; the wealthiest 10 percent receive 40 percent of national income. The counterpart to this concentration of income in the hands of the wealthy is found at the other end of the income scale in Latin America: the poorest 30 percent of the population receive only 7.5 percent of total income, less than anywhere else in the world.

These bald statistics are arrived at from an analysis of household surveys from fourteen countries that account for more than 80 percent of the region's populations. The surveys were done between 1994 and 1996. Sample sizes were large: in Peru, for example, 16,744 households were queried, providing data about 88,863 Peruvians. Data from these surveys were compared to data from earlier surveys, too, leading to the sober conclusion that inequality in Latin America worsened considerably in the 1980s and has remained stagnant at high levels in the 1990s.

Finally, comparisons with other parts of the world are facilitated by international databases prepared by such organizations as the World Bank and the International Monetary Fund.

The Inter-American Development Bank report not only goes to unprecedented lengths to measure rigorously inequality in Latin America, but also documents its deadly implication: widespread poverty. The income level of more than 150 million Latin Americans—roughly a third of the population—is under two dollars a day (corrected for differences of purchasing power of the currencies of the various countries). And two dollars is the meager sum regarded as the minimum needed to cover basic consumption needs. Thus, although the World Bank and the International Monetary Fund judge the per capita incomes of Latin America to be high enough to warrant the region being labeled "middle-income," a third of the population barely subsists.

The economists who authored the study acknowledge that there is inequality everywhere. But they say that Latin America has *excess* inequality. Other regions with similar levels of "development" have substantially less poverty. If Latin America had the income distribution level suited to its level of development by international standards, the incidence of poverty would be half of what it actually is today. Per capita income levels of eastern European countries are not appreciably different from those of Latin America, but only 7 percent of their population are poor. Admittedly, the socialist history of Eastern Europe strains the comparison. Still, comparisons with other regions of the world lead to a similar conclusion. For example, if income in Latin America were distributed as it is in the countries of Southeast Asia, poverty in Latin America would be reduced by four-fifths.

Actually, income distribution in Latin America is surely even worse than calculated by the Inter-American Development Bank study. The household surveys measure only income from labor, not capital (such as rental properties and other kinds of investments). Revenue from investments is an important source of income for the wealthy. The measurement of income from labor and other data from the household surveys, though, provides insight into the wealthy of Latin America. The wealthy are numerous, a class, not a clan of tight-knit families. The wealthy are well educated, working as professionals and managers of companies (in which they may, or may not, have equity). Wives tend to work, and to earn a good income. Families are small, with an average of just 1.4 children.

The poor have a poor education. Twenty-three percent of Latin Americans are held to be "uneducated." The average Latin American over twenty-five years of age has only 4.8 years of education. Three-fourths of Latin Americans over twenty-five years of age have no education or, more likely today, only a number of years in a primary (elementary) school. It is the poor who never make it to school or attend school only for a few years. The households of the poor are larger; the poorest 30 percent of Latin Americans have an average of 6.3 members in their household. The poor have more children, an average of 3.3. And households are more likely to include additional adult dependents (such as grandparents). Hence, per capita income is lower for poor families not only because earnings are less, but also because they have more individuals to support.

Most of the poor still live in the countryside. Only in Brazil, Chile, and Venezuela do more than half of all households of the poorest 30 percent live in urban areas. The urban slums of the poor can be even more depressing—and dangerous—than the forsaken rural settlements of the poor, but again it is notable that the majority of the poor continue to live in the countryside. In contrast, nine out of ten families in the two highest income deciles live in cities.

Left unexamined in the report is the life of the poor. But then how can you convey a sense for what it means to be poor, and moreover for 150 million Latin Americans? My own scattered conversations with the poor of the region lead me to believe that any attempt has to include more than a description of the misery and wretchedness. Poverty entails, too, emotional pressures, for example, of fear and worry. Sometimes there is despair, humiliation, or rage. Poverty is profoundly threatening. It takes a constant toll on one's equilibrium and frequently, too, on family ties. Finally, the burden of poverty is different—and greater— for the inequality that is always so evident—so transparent—in Latin America. The munificence of the few is a constant reminder that life could be more bountiful. Moreover, the wealthy, as employers, are frequently demanding, miserly, and insensitive. The poor do have their "weapons of the weak": false compliance, dissimulation, foot-dragging, and sabotage. There is a never-ending struggle in what James Scott has called "the small arms fire of class war." The social landscape among classes in Latin America is treacherous.

Why is Latin America so inequitable? The economists who authored the Inter-American Development Bank study offer two theories, but neither is very persuasive. One explanation proffered is that Latin America is at an early "stage of economic development" where, for example, a scarcity of capital leads to high returns, which are a cause of income inequality. But as capital becomes more abundant, its returns fall vis-à-vis labor, helping to improve income distribution. Similarly, the present low levels of schooling entail high returns for the few who are educated. So with continued economic growth, the expansion of education, and other good things, the distribution of income should improve. This line of reasoning sounds plausible. But empirical studies have concluded that when countries, such as the Philippines, begin with inequality, after several decades of economic growth they remain inegalitarian. This outcome does not seem surprising. It also fits the experience of Latin America. At the beginning of the twentieth century, Latin America was inegalitarian. After a century of economic growth, it is still inegalitarian. Why should another half century of unfettered economic activity, or even another century, lead—by itself—to a reversal?

Another explanation for Latin America's inequality—and by extension for the poverty of so many Latin Americans—is the region's endowment of natural resources. This explanation is surprising. But evidence is marshaled to show that countries near the equator have systematically higher income inequality, even after accounting for lower levels of economic development than countries in temperate regions. This relationship is true throughout the world, and Latin America is not an exception. Similarly, countries with large amounts of agricultural land per capita are substantially more unequal than countries with little land per capita. Furthermore, countries that rely upon large exports of primary commodities are also substantially more unequal than countries with lower primary commodity exports. But it is hard to believe that abundance is a burden, or that there is something pernicious about either tropical fruits (including coffee) or the equator. What is missing from the analysis is an appreciation of the politics of inequality.

Neither of these two possible explanations is pushed very far. The bankers and economists of the Inter-American Development Bank do not appear really interested in explaining the cause of inequality in Latin America. In any case, solutions do not leap from their analysis. Latin America's severe income inequality is connected to its level of development and to the characteristics of its natural resource endowment. That would seem to provide a twofold reason for doing nothing: the first implies waiting and the second resignation.

But fitting an institution which is often referred to as a "international development organization," an organization committed to fostering "development," the spirit of the Inter-American Development Bank report is in suggesting *policies* that can reduce income inequality. And redress is to come from the state: "Income distribution in Latin American countries will depend heavily on government in the next century."

The logic of the officials of the Inter-American Development Bank is curious. In explaining the cause of inequality, they look to distant, impersonal, exogenous variables: the "stage of development" and natural resource endowment. Slighted are issues of authority and power. Those who have long held the reins of power in Latin America, of the economy and of the state, are not held accountable. But if the serious problem of inequality—and the poverty it begets—is to be redressed, then, yes, it is necessary to look at the management of the economy and of the state.

During the economic recession that battered Latin America in the 1980s, which was the worst since the 1930s, "international development organizations" had considerable leverage over policy design and implementation in Latin America. There were four powerful institutions, all based in Washington: the World Bank, the International Monetary Fund (IMF), the Inter-American Development Bank, and the United States Agency for International Development (AID). In what came to be known as the "Washington consensus," there was a pitch for Latin American governments to attain macroeconomic stability. Key was reining in government deficits, which had long fueled inflation. Government spending was slashed, and to a lesser extent, taxes were raised. Likewise, the four institutions promoted economic "liberalization," ending government intervention in the economy to leave markets "free." Since many government interventions, such as maintaining unprofitable state enterprises or offering subsidies to consumers, added to budget deficits, "liberalization" was seen as contributing to fiscal responsibility. But trade policy was also "liberalized," as were controls on foreign investment. These latter measures were said to contribute handsomely to economic growth.

The pressing financial needs of Latin American governments gave credit-bearing, international organizations considerable leverage. But Latin Americans policy makers, beaten down by debt and inflation, were in any case receptive to a new paradigm. The old statist model was thoroughly discredited in the 1980s. In country after country, when there was a change of political regime—and sometimes even before— central bankers and finance ministers pursued the prescriptions of the "international donor community." And, poof, they worked: macroeconomic stability (a euphemism for low rates of inflation) was attained throughout the region, even in countries, such as Brazil, Bolivia, and Nicaragua, that had been wracked by hyperinflation.

But the policy prescriptions of fiscal restraint and economic "liberalization" appear to have been "oversold": throughout Latin America many came to believe that the prescriptions would be a panacea for all economic woes, including the poverty afflicting a third of Latin Americans. Throughout the 1990s Latin American countries, on average, enjoyed moderate (if inconsistent) rates of economic growth. Nonetheless, as the Inter-American Development Bank report acknowledges, income distribution has not improved. The poor remain poor. Economic growth was an inadequate remedy.

So the World Bank, the Inter-American Development Bank, and

other similar international organizations call for a "second generation" of reforms to help address pressing social needs: education, health care, and income generation for the poor. Public opinion surveys by Latinobarómetro suggest that Latin Americans are supportive of these kinds of reforms. For example, at least four out of five Latin Americans think that government has a responsibility to "reduce the differences between the rich and the poor." An even higher percentage of Latin Americans thinks that government ought to accept responsibility for "providing health care to the sick" as well as "a decent standard of living" for old people and the unemployed. A philosophical endorsement of ambitious government efforts to provide redress for the poor of Latin America comes from an essay by Mario Vargas Llosa titled "América Latina y la opción liberal." He makes a forceful argument that liberal democracy and capitalism is defensible only if there is equal opportunity for all. Especially important, he suggests, is equality before the law and equal opportunities in education. Vargas Llosa laments that much more needs to be done before all Latin Americans have anything close to an equal opportunity for personal advancement.

International development organizations such as the Inter-American Development Bank make a well-reasoned case for social reform in Latin America. And the majority of Latin Americans appear to endorse at least the idea of these reforms. But despite occasional rhetoric to the contrary, little is being done to redress income inequality by providing needed social services—education in particular—that might help the poor improve their welfare. The so-called second generation reforms are not forthcoming. Government and economic elites are distracted by the continuing struggle to maintain macroeconomic stability. Also, the challenge of meeting the needs of the poor is daunting. A Herculean effort is necessary, and no government has an abundance of political capital. Most of the region's presidents—and their cabinets—do little more than lurch from one crisis to another. But, unfortunately, there also does not seem to be sufficient empathy for the poor. The chasm among classes is huge.

In the world's richest countries (which tend to have a more equitable distribution of income), government spending represents around 40 percent of gross domestic product (GDP). In contrast, Latin America, with the world's worst distribution of income, is also the region where governments are smallest. Government spending in Latin America represents about 20 percent of GDP. The scope of government in the region is constrained by difficulties in taxing those who have something that might be taxed. Indeed, income tax rates in Latin America are the lowest in the world. The Inter-American Development Bank suggests that "low collection rates for income and other taxes in Latin America reflect the limited institutional capacity of public administration to enforce the law." That interpretation has merit, but it needs to be complemented by an understanding of the political constraints to strengthening the capacity of the public sector, especially for collecting taxes to aid the poor.

To be sure, throughout Latin America there are programs to aid the poor. But so often they pale before the challenge. And when efforts are ambitious, all too often they are driven by political calculations. For example, with only a year to go before standing for reelection in 1995 as president of Peru—an opportunity made possible only by rewriting the constitution—Alberto Fujimori suddenly embarked upon a dramatic expansion of government social spending. Fujimori profited politically by having the media portray him, wearing a poncho, visiting remote Andean communities to inaugurate schools or other "public works." The political manipulation of social spending, much of it financed by the sale of state assets, was blatant. It was, as is said in Latin America, "*un* show." Mexico's Programa Nacional de Solidaridad has been similarly criticized.

The Inter-American Development Bank report for 1998–1999 highlights the importance of improving access to education for reducing inequality in Latin America. It is true that slowly the poor of Latin America are becoming better educated. Illiteracy is being eradicated, and the average number of years of schooling is slowly being increased. But the real dynamism in education in Latin America is in the growth of professional training for the sons and daughters of the elite. Many of today's professionals, those who garner the high wages, are children whose parents enjoyed a comfortable status from their investments in agriculture, industry, commerce, or construction. Here is a story the report does not tell. The upper class of Latin America has a remarkable gift for self-preservation and has been quick to realize that in our era the most valuable—and the safest—capital is human capital. Meeting the need for quality higher education are many new private universities, found throughout the major cities of the region. They are good, they are expensive, and they are most definitely not agencies of equality.

# Chapter 11

## Struggling for Gender Equality

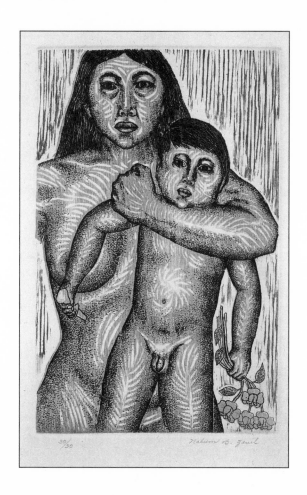

I N MEXICO there is an expression, "The dog is master of the cat, the cat is master of the mouse, and the mouse is master of its tail."

During a lunch in the Bronx with an academic from the Dominican Republic, Milagros Ricourt, I mentioned that I was taken by how Puerto Ricans often complain of discrimination in the United States, but that they, in turn, often made deprecatory remarks about Dominicans. I recounted, too, that when I asked a Puerto Rican graduate student at Princeton University why Puerto Ricans commonly denigrate Dominicans, she simply rubbed her skin, which I understood to be an allusion to the "African heritage" of many Dominicans. But, I continued, there is such a record of discrimination in the Dominican Republic toward Haitians, again based overwhelmingly on race. "Yes," said Milagros, nodding in agreement, "but it doesn't end there. In Haiti, the family dog is at the bottom."

A year later, in San Salvador, Deysi Cheyne filled in the gap. "There is so much violence and such a pronounced hierarchy in the family. The father comes home drunk and beats his wife. She slaps her eldest son. He hits his younger brother. And the little boy kicks the dog." Deysi is the director of the Institute for Research, Training, and Development of Women, a nongovernmental organization in El Salvador. She and her organization, known by its Spanish acronym, IMU, strive to improve the welfare of the women of El Salvador, a heroic undertaking, but one that Deysi finds more satisfying and productive than any other endeavor. This commitment stems in part from her identification with the plight of women, but also in part from her disillusionment with party politics and the workings of El Salvador's incipient democracy.

Deysi is doing good work, but her attitude toward politics illustrates how many "on the left" in Latin America have gone from an all-consuming passion for seizing the state to a virtual abandonment of interest in government. Party politics, electoral politics, and the slow labor of democratic governance and democratic opposition are frequently dismissed—as if there is no middle ground between creating a Leninist state and retreating to the barrio.

Deysi grew up in the provincial city of La Libertad. As a college student at the University of El Salvador (commonly called the national university) she was, as she says, "recruited" by the Salvadoran Communist Party (PCS). A scholarship enabled her to study biology in Moldavia, part of the former Soviet Union. The university, in the capital city of Kishinev, was at that time named Moldavian V. I. Lenin State University. Her studies in biology were complemented by training in "intelligence gathering and analysis." Learning Russian was a formidable challenge, but one that she mastered. Moldavia impressed her with its egalitarian society, but she also found it stifling. A friend expressed to her the frustration of local artists: "wanting to paint like Pablo Picasso but being forced to paint 'social realism.'"

After four years of study in Moldavia, from 1976 to 1980, Deysi returned to El Salvador, where she participated in clandestine activities of the Salvadoran Communist Party, one of the oldest Communist parties in Latin America, having been founded in 1930. The triumph of the Sandinistas in neighboring Nicaragua gave the "left" in El Salvador impetus for pushing for a similar revolution. But the repression by the armed forces and the police was savage. It was a most dangerous period.

In 1983 Deysi was sent to Nicaragua, where she did intelligence work for the Farabundo Martí National Liberation Front (FMLN), which the Communist Party had joined in 1980, though it continued to maintain, too, an independent party structure. Deysi describes her work in Nicaragua, where she stayed for six years, as mundane, preparing intelligence reports for the "general staff" of the FMLN. During this period of intense conflict in El Salvador, Deysi lived in Managua, far from the battles between the Sandinistas and the counterrevolutionaries (the *contra*). Still, Deysi witnessed the divisions and hardships that accompanied the Nicaraguan Revolution. She did not waiver, though, in her wish to see a similar revolution in El Salvador.

Ten days before the "final offensive" of 1989, Deysi returned to El Salvador, traveling on a false passport. Crossing the border between Honduras and El Salvador was the height of anxiety: discovery of her true identity, or just that her passport was false, would result, she assumed, in immediate death. The final offensive in San Salvador was ghastly, with many of her colleagues killed, mostly at close quarters. The offensive was not successful, though it may well have convinced the army that they were far from winning the war and so contributed to the negotiation of a peace agreement. That settlement did not come until 1992; in the intervening period Deysi lived in constant danger.

In 1992 Deysi assumed the responsibility of leadership of the IMU. It had been founded in 1986 by colleagues in the FMLN to raise the political awareness of women, to help them in their daily struggles, and to marshal their support for the insurrection. The woman who contributed the most to the founding of the IMU, Norma Guirola, was captured during the final offensive. Her burned body, barely identifiable, was found in a field at the end of the ordeal. However, the IMU, surely suspect to the authorities, survived and continued its work.

At the close of the war, Deysi was a member of the Central Committee of the Salvadoran Communist Party (PSC), with an additional title, Responsible to the Secretariat for the Welfare of Women. The PSC jockeyed with other parties and groups to define a new identity for the

FMLN, which moved from being a clandestine guerrilla organization to a political party, competing in elections alongside its former "enemies." But Deysi has become disenchanted with party politics, and she remains suspicious of democracy itself. And she is still "anticapitalist." For her, "We have elections, we have democracy, but when I go out into the streets I see poverty. The economy is reported to be growing at a healthy rate of such-and-such, but when I go out into the streets I see more poverty. I don't see that democracy with its attendant economic system is improving the lives of poor people. It has made no difference to most people." Deysi no longer believes revolution is a viable solution to El Salvador's problems, but she also is not convinced that voting for this party or for that party in elections will accomplish much. Deysi feels it is necessary to go straight to the disenfranchised, to work directly with them, to "help them help themselves."

In 1995 the different political parties that made up the FMLN dissolved their respective party structures to become just "currents" or "tendencies" within a revamped FMLN. The move was to strengthen the FMLN and to enhance its electoral possibilities. I sense that for Deysi the attendant loss of her party responsibilities was a relief, allowing her to spend more time with the activities of the IMU and its "grassroots" work with poor women.

The IMU occupies a spacious house in San Salvador that was bought for little money during the civil war from a scared member of the "bourgeoisie." Like nearly every other house in the neighborhood, it is surrounded by a high wall (for "security"). Inside the house is a warren of offices for the staff of thirty-two, all of whom are women except the guard and the two chauffeurs (who also, in a sense, serve as guards, especially in the isolated rural areas where Deysi and her colleagues frequently travel). In the front of the house, instead of a baroque fountain of a cherub, is a somber, concrete memorial to women who lost their lives during the insurrection.

The mission statement of IMU is: "Raise awareness in El Salvador of the discrimination and subordination of women, promote measures that enhance the status of women, strengthen the organization of women, and encourage the political and social participation of women at both the community and national level." A poster produced by the IMU is more specific. It states:

Platform of the Women of El Salvador
Fifty-Two Percent of the Population Demand:

1. A halt to incest, rape, and sexual molestation.
2. Land, credit, and technical assistance for women.
3. Decent housing, with ownership, for women.
4. Job training, employment, and equal salaries.

5. A halt to increases in the cost of basic foodstuffs.
6. Equality of opportunity for girls in schools.
7. Comprehensive health care for women in more and better hospitals.
8. Comprehensive sexual education and sexuality without prejudices.
9. Free and voluntary maternity.
10. Responsible paternity.
11. Respect for the environment and a better quality of life for women.
12. Social policies that meet the needs of women.
13. Nondiscriminatory laws.
14. Fifty percent of the positions of power for women.

Prodding El Salvador to meet these demands is a daunting challenge.

Research conducted by the staff of IMU shows that the average number of years in school for women in El Salvador is only three years. Men are also poorly educated, but their average number of years in school is four. Only 2.7 percent of men study in a university, but for women the figure is even less, a mere 0.7 percent. Public health is deemed to neglect the needs of women. There is only one public maternity hospital in the country. Despite high rates of breast and uterus cancer in El Salvador, there is no effort by public health authorities to detect cases early so that treatment is possible. Economically, too, women suffer from discrimination. It is estimated that women receive, on average, salaries 30 percent less than men for the same work. Also suggestive is that only 12 percent of the titles awarded in the recent agrarian reform were given to women. Likewise, despite active political participation throughout the history of El Salvador, women have been shunned at the top, and few hold positions of authority. Presidents and cabinet members are almost always men. In Congress only 10 percent of representatives are women. The judicial system, too, lacks women in ranking positions.

But it is research on violence against women that is most alarming in its findings. For example, a survey suggested that 57 percent of women at least on occasion suffer from physical abuse in their household, from violence committed by their spouses. Furthermore, in marriages there are often problems of sexual mistreatment and psychological intimidation. Another study concluded that 51 percent of working women have experienced sexual harassment in the workplace. It is estimated that only 5 percent of rapes in the country are reported, which in and of itself is judged to be an indictment of the acceptance in the country of violence against women. The consequences of this violence against women, so much of which happens just within the family, are enormous, contributing to low self-esteem, depression, emotional insecurity, and constant fear.

The division of labor within the family is also a source of concern. Research sponsored by the IMU on women living in rural areas reveals that women commonly work outside the home yet shoulder nearly all household and child-rearing chores. Consequently, rural women routinely labor a daunting fourteen to eighteen hours per day. Surveys of women residing in San Salvador, now home to a fourth of the population of El Salvador, reveal a similar pattern. In 95 percent of families women prepare all meals, in 90 percent of families women wash all clothes, in 84 percent of families women take children to receive medical attention, and so forth. One of IMU's publications has a drawing of a woman doubled over from holding a boulder labeled "patriarchy." On top of the boulder sits a man sipping a cup of coffee.

The IMU contributes to solving the problems particular to women in El Salvador through a variety of projects. There are community-based projects, such as the construction of a nutrition center in an isolated village, which women manage for the benefit of their children. Similarly, there are projects that seek to assist women and their families by halting environmental degradation in vulnerable communities; retaining walls are built, and areas are reforested. Campaigns are mounted against degrading portrayals of women in advertising campaigns. Research on women is undertaken, and the findings are published. Most common, though, are diverse but persistent efforts to raise awareness among women about their inherent rights and to urge them to organize themselves so that they can make claims on state and society for the fulfillment of these rights.

Funding for the projects and general activities of the IMU comes overwhelmingly from foreign assistance, especially from the Netherlands and Sweden. Foreign institutions have been charitable, but seemingly everywhere there are cutbacks in foreign aid and, also, more restrictions on how assistance can be used, and more laborious reporting requirements. Deysi spends a considerable amount of time looking for funding and ensuring that the needs of donors are satisfied. And working with foreign assistance means that the IMU is at least somewhat hostage to the trends—or fads—among the "donor community." A project that might be favorably received one year may seem dull the next year. One has to do good work, but one also has to "market" it well. As the director of the organization, Deysi has many responsibilities, one of the most taxing of which is just managing different constituents.

At times, Deysi's work takes her to the reaches of the state, and I sense that here she is less comfortable, or perhaps just suspicious. For example, in 1996 El Salvador's Congress passed a law creating a new institute, supported by the government: the Salvadoran Institute for the Progress of Women (ISDEMU). The institute was given the task of "formulating, implementing, and ensuring the fulfillment of national policies toward women." The "board of directors" includes four representatives of nongovernmental organizations dedicated to promoting the welfare of women. The IMU was elected to the board of directors. Other directors are six ministers of state: justice, education, labor, health and social welfare, agriculture, and public safety. The president chooses the overall director. President Armando Calderón Sol selected his wife, Elizabeth de Calderón Sol. She is unmistakably from the "bourgeoisie," and thus represents what Deysi had risked her life to overthrow, to hurl into the graveyard of history. But Elizabeth de Calderón Sol has an interest and a commitment to the welfare of women. She is intelligent, and in the end she is a woman, too, and so undeniably aware of what women of all classes in El Salvador endure. Deysi decided to give her—and the new state institute—the benefit of the doubt and to see if together they could not push ahead the collective interests of Salvadoran women. Still, Deysi is determined that the brunt of her work, and the work of the IMU, will continue to be directly with the poor and the subordinate of El Salvador.

In pursuing her work, Deysi is calm and soft-spoken, not betraying the drive that led her to ascend the ranks of the Communist Party of El Salvador, the fear she lived with throughout El Salvador's civil war, or the misery and death she has seen. But when I asked her if the past all seems like a dream, she said, "no." Like many revolutionaries of her generation, she missed the opportunity to have a family of her own. She has no children, although she has a *compañero*." When asked about his sensitivity to gender issues, she laughs and says, "he tries to understand." Deysi is surprised though—and perhaps sometimes even overwhelmed—by how much the parameters of politics have changed in El Salvador, and, she feels, "It is so much harder now that there is no model to serve as a guide and as a vision." But, unfortunately, what has not changed are the serious problems besetting El Salvador, one of the poorest and most inegalitarian countries of Latin America. The cover of one of IMU's trimester bulletins has the title, "Before, During, and After the War: The Culture Is the Same." In the title, "culture" is understood to refer to gender constructs and practices, but the same persistence can be observed in many of the ills plaguing El Salvador, above all the stubborn poverty of the country. Deysi feels she is tackling one ill directly, that her energies are not dissipated in internecine party disputes, election posturing, or in a lumbering bureaucracy.

In the summer of 1999, Deysi was approached by the leadership of the FMLN and asked if she would be willing to be one of the party's candidates in the congressional elections of March 2000. She declined the offer.

Others in Latin America, who like Deysi aspire to see a better world, have also elected to sidestep what used to be the all-consuming passion—class divisions—and to focus, instead, on other important issues, such as environmental degradation, local governance, health care, education, and gender. Similarly, there is also the realization that control of the state is not the only means to evoke change. One can work directly with society, strengthening abilities for self-governance, reshaping cultural practices, or other diverse goals. The demise of Marxism in Latin America has left a big ideological hole (into which many have just disappeared), but it has also allowed for a broader, more encompassing political agenda and permitted a more eclectic array of strategies for pursing social change.

Some perceive that the political work, the social activism, of the kind pursued by Deysi and her colleagues at the IMU is the seed for a future challenge to the liberal paradigm in Latin America. These "social movements," as they are frequently called, are part of the "political landscape" throughout the region. And they frequently are able to make a difference in the lives of those whom they reach. But by eschewing the state, and in avoiding the challenge of fomenting an overarching understanding of how state and society could be reconfigured, they confine themselves to local issues and—ultimately—to political marginalization.

Even for narrow political goals—such as the empowerment of women—it can be asked, How reasonable is it to skip the state? Despite the fashion for "lean government" in this liberal era, the state still has vast resources—including authority. Why, for example, ignore the Ministry of Health, the Ministry of Education, and even the police? Could not more be accomplished if, through political participation, these institutions are made more efficient, more responsive? Ministries are elephantine and lumbering, but it is unlikely that their responsibilities are going to be met by small (or even large) nongovernmental organizations dependent on foreign assistance. The Salvadoran state is unlikely to respond to the needs of the poor majority, and women in particular, unless it is politically directed to fulfill this need.

Despite misgivings about the potential reach of the IMU, I respect Deysi and the work she does for the women of El Salvador. And it is understandable how she could conclude there is nothing more useful than the work she is doing and no better way to do it than by reaching out directly to women.

In the window of a bookstore in Guatemala I saw a small poster, showing a rooster and a hen. Beneath them was scrawled, *"Tu serás muy gallo pero la que pone los huevos soy yo."* A not-so-literal translation: "You are a big cock, but I'm the one that lays the eggs." I asked and received permission to make a copy of the poster, which I did at a small shop down the street. I sent it to Deysi.

# Chapter 12

## *El Gringo*

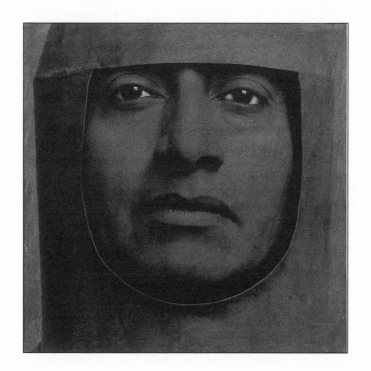

Nᴇᴀʀʟʏ ᴇᴠᴇʀʏᴏɴᴇ, it seems, knows *el gringo*, the nickname of uncertain origin for the North American, sometimes used, too, for Europeans (much to their annoyance). Even if a *gringo* is not known personally, every Latin American knows at least the role he plays and has some exaggerated view of who he—and it usually is a male—is. When not just a slovenly tourist, *el gringo* plays the role of the *expert*, the conduit for the transmittal of technology, of arcane but useful knowledge, of the cultural avant-garde, of spiritual redemption, and of other wonders of the United States (and Canada). *El gringo* brings earthmoving equipment, agrochemicals, instructions on how to run a McDonald's franchise, advice on how to run an election campaign, music television, skills to repair Boeing aircraft, gold-mining equipment, aid in combating international trade in narcotics, pharmaceuticals, recommendations on how to privatize state enterprises, help in becoming a Mormon . . . the list is seemingly endless. The influence of the United States upon Latin America is considerable and pervasive. With the passage of time, the influence of the United States is, perhaps, less heavy-handed, but if anything it is even more ubiquitous, creeping not just into politics and finance, but into every nook of life in the region, including culture.

Just how North Americans come to exert influence upon Latin Americans is complicated. The diffusion of ideas and norms, of goods and services, often evokes resistance, and often, too, involves a transformation, a retailoring of what is offered to suit local needs and tastes. Or the "terms" under which something is offered are contested. Still, a defining characteristic of Latin America as a region is that it is very much influenced by a neighboring region, by North America. But little attention is, ordinarily, called to this influence. This foreign influence is not hidden, but because it is often invited or at least "negotiated," it appears less offensive. And at other times, the influence of the United States is just viewed as a generic—and so harmless—"modernization." Still, the relationship between *el gringo* and Latin American society is always complicated, fraught with ambiguities and fears that reflect an imbalance of power and the sensibilities of nationalism.

One of the protagonists of the Mexican art renaissance illustrates well the influence of the "outsider," of *el gringo:* William Spratling. He does not deserve to be forgotten or trivialized with a banal hagiography. The latter appears to be the greatest threat. Tour books of Mexico are not alone in eulogizing him as the North American who designed beautiful silver jewelry with pre-Columbian motifs in Taxco and willy-nilly revived the city's silver industry, who befriended Diego Rivera, Miguel Covarrubias, David Siqueiros, and other Mexican artists of the day, and who was a renowned collector of—and authority on—pre-Columbian art. Buttressing this rosy image, at one corner of Taxco's plaza is the

Calle Guillermo Spratling with its bust of Spratling, and just behind the Santa Prisca Cathedral is the William Spratling Museum, filled with pieces from his pre-Columbian art collection. Such a benevolent image of William Spratling, though, masks the colorfulness of his personal life, his discreditable trading in pre-Columbian fakes, his conflict with his adopted Mexican society, and, most important, the intricacies and ironies of his contribution to the flowering of Mexican art in the aftermath of the Mexican Revolution.

Spratling's silver jewelry and small table objects are truly beautiful. Spratling-designed pieces sold in such well-heeled stores as Tiffany, Saks Fifth Avenue, and Neiman-Marcus. They were purchased by everyone from Emperor Haile Selassie to Orson Welles, and are avidly collected today. By reverently employing Olmec and Aztec designs in his silver, Spratling was part of a larger artistic movement that pictorially celebrated and embellished what was indigenous to Mexico. Spratling's knowledge of contemporary artistic trends, of art deco and of the work of Danish designers, ensured that while he drew upon Mexico's pre-Columbian artistic legacy, the silver objects he created were decidedly modern.

Yet Spratling's most significant part in the Mexican art renaissance has to be his promotion of this renaissance in the United States (and by extension, Europe). The articles on Mexican artists that Spratling wrote in the late 1920s for the *Herald Tribune* and the *New York Times* helped solidify and boost the careers of the artists. In 1930 Spratling persuaded the American ambassador to commission Diego Rivera to paint a mural at the Cortés Palace in Cuernavaca. Spratling's delightful book, *Little Mexico*, published in 1932 (with a foreword by Diego Rivera), furthered North American interest in Mexico. Also, Spratling's silver business, which at its zenith employed four hundred craftsmen, attracted publicity. But most decisive of all was Spratling himself, a colorful character who became a celebrity. While he had notable friends like William Faulkner before he moved to Mexico, in Mexico he was visited by such personalities as Bette Davis and Paulette Goddard.

Chasing the perceived tastes of successful authors and celebrities were industrialists and financiers with money to buy expensive paintings and busloads of tourists to buy "folk art." The Mexican art renaissance was profoundly nationalist and populist, but nonetheless an ironic symbiosis existed between the artists and North American and European collectors. Foreign appreciation and demand encouraged and emboldened Mexican artists. Moreover, their standing in Mexican society undoubtedly was strengthened by the respect they commanded abroad and in the expatriate community in Mexico.

As a North American living in Mexico, as a writer, as an artisan celebrating indigenous Mexican art, as a friend of important Mexican artists, and above all as a self-created personality, Spratling was a vital link between Mexico and the United States. Spratling's colorful, brazen lifestyle was instrumental in enabling him to play his appointed role in the Mexican art renaissance. Spratling was an engaging raconteur, with wide experiences to draw upon, including traveling in the rugged Mexican state of Guerrero and mishaps with his planes and boats.

The ranch outside Taxco that he retreated to had tropical fruit trees, flower gardens, pre-Columbian stone artifacts, and a small zoo. There was a pool with the stipulation that no bathing suits be worn in it. Spratling was a homosexual with a fondness for muscular young men, which he did not go to great lengths to conceal. He was a chain-smoker and, beginning in the afternoon, a hard drinker.

Spratling's relationship with the Mexican society he helped enliven and promote abroad was not as harmonious as the casual visitor to Taxco today is led to believe. According to Spratling's former employees, Spratling was honest, straightforward, and generous. He took care to train his workers in a variety of skills. And above all he is venerated for creating work in a community where employment was scarce. For Tomás Vega García, who started working for Spratling when he was only eight, Spratling alone deserves credit for Taxco's present prosperity.

Surprisingly, Spratling's homosexuality was met with shrug-of-the-shoulders generosity by his workers and the population of Taxco, then a small, Catholic town. His former workers still laugh at the memory of how Spratling required them to strip before they would swim in his pool after the day's work was finished.

However, while Spratling enjoyed harmonious relations with his workers, with the town of Taxco itself a rift developed. Indeed, for the last twenty years of his life Spratling avoided Taxco, taking care of his needs in the anything but picturesque town of Iguala instead. Except for twice, Spratling did not even attend Taxco's annual silver fair—which was held in his honor.

The rift between Spratling and Taxco had many roots. The most immediate appears to have been a quarrel over changing the date for the annual silver fair. There was also resentment at the wealth and success of the "outsider," aggravated because he was a North American. Spratling, in turn, may have tired of the many requests he reportedly received for "contributions" to community welfare. But the real source of friction was that so many silversmiths in Taxco, including many that Spratling himself had trained, shamelessly copied his designs. Some even copied the stamp of his workshop, passing off their silver as Spratling silver.

It is difficult to know if the copying of his work posed meaningful financial competition to Spratling or if it just offended his sense of artistic integrity. The copying of his work became so common, though, that when an employee announced he was leaving Spratling's workshop, Spratling would unfailingly say, "I wish you well, but please don't copy me." Imitation, though, was inevitable with the absence of employment opportunities in the area surrounding Taxco, the increasing number of tourists flush with dollars, and the popularity of Spratling's silver.

As much as Spratling resented the copying of his own "art," he himself gave in to the same temptations with pre-Columbian art. Spratling's fascination with pre-Columbian art appears to have begun with his arrival in Mexico. It developed throughout his years in Mexico and was a constant source of inspiration for his silver designs. He thus was like Diego Rivera, Miguel Covarrubias, and Rufino Tamayo, who all appreciated pre-Columbian art, collected it, and found in it artistic inspiration. In his autobiography, *File on Spratling*, Spratling discusses going down to Iguala with Miguel Covarrubias to buy pre-Columbian artifacts:

> It was good hunting then, and we had to take along baskets which, like as not, we could fill up in the course of a couple of hours. The pieces were rude and heavy, occasionally highly polished, a few very fine, but the major part of material available were rather coarse examples of stone sculpture. These were pieces, some of which, having been exchanged later, found their way to New York galleries . . . and even European galleries, where they enjoyed considerable vogue and where, of course, their prices increased more than a thousandfold.

Spratling often swapped pre-Columbian material with Diego Rivera, offering the great painter material from Guerrero in exchange for objects from the central Valley of Mexico. Also, Spratling donated many objects from his collection to the National University of Mexico and to the Museum of Anthropology and History.

The Mexican art renaissance contributed decisively to the fashion for collecting pre-Columbian art and a corresponding spiral in prices of pre-Columbian artifacts. As Spratling noted in his autobiography, "Sources of material brought to the collectors have their roots among the provincial poor, among which are to be found the ingenuous, at the same time very clever, rogues." Demand from affluent city folk for "coarse examples of stone sculpture" led the rural poor, and the not so poor and not so rural, to begin fashioning copies—fakes—of pre-Columbian artifacts. Diego Rivera himself would sometimes be duped into buying fake pre-Columbian ceramics. When informed of the duplicity, he had a nonchalant reply: "Same clay. Same Indians." Others, though, were not as forgiving.

While there is no evidence that Spratling was a party to the production of fakes, toward the end of his life he appears to have caved in to the temptation to pass on, at a sizable profit to himself, some of the fakes made in Guerrero to wealthy visitors to his ranch. Some of his generation's most prominent collectors were, to their dismay, tricked. Those who knew Spratling well have different interpretations for why the man who complained so bitterly about being copied in Taxco sometimes sold expensive pre-Columbian fakes. One interpretation is that toward the end of his life he was drinking so heavily that he could no longer tell what was genuine and what was fake. Others believe that he was always one for practical jokes. In his freezer, for example, he kept cement disguised to look like ice cream. And he had lead poured three-fourths of the way up coffee cups; he would add a little coffee and serve the cups to guests with the notice that "this is very heavy coffee." From these practical jokes came guessing games about what was real and what was not.

The more persistent explanation is that Spratling could not pass up the opportunity to make easy money from people he did not necessarily respect. Spratling is said "to have not been indifferent to money" and, indeed, to have had a nose for sniffing out those who had a great deal of money. Perhaps, too, that wave of interest in the Mexican renaissance, which he himself had helped generate, became a bit tiring and so worthy of exploitation. Similarly, there are stories of how in his later years Diego Rivera would sometimes charge exorbitant fees for painting the portraits of foreign visitors, usually from the United States. He would invite the foreigners to his studio and then proceed to paint caricatures of them.

Spratling was killed in a car accident in August of 1967. He was making an early morning trip to Mexico City when his car crashed into a tree that a storm the night before had blown across the road. At the time of his death he was bankrupt, his silver business was in disorder, and he was drinking heavily. His loyal workers took turns carrying the coffin to the little cemetery, and thousands of people crowded the ceremony.

Perhaps it is fitting that today in the William Spratling Museum in Taxco there are both pre-Columbian artifacts and "reproductions." Sometimes objects are labeled, enabling the visitor to tell what is genuine and what is not. But other times there are no labels, and the curious have to guess what is real and what is not. Ironically, the museum does not have a single piece of Spratling's silver on exhibition, although the museum is surrounded by shops selling silver jewelry and objects inspired by Spratling. In the museum there is only a single picture of its namesake, taken with Miguel Covarrubias. It is inconspicuously hung upstairs on the second floor. Above the picture is a caption obliquely criticizing private collections of pre-Columbian art. For those not familiar with William Spratling's life, the museum is a little jarring. But actually, everything is in harmony.

There continue to be many North Americans visiting or residing in Latin America who reshape the pliable region. But there are other ways, too, in which the United States influences Latin America: movies, television (including music television), music, the Internet, trade, the Fulbright program (which sponsors the exchange of scholars), diplomatic machinations, foreign aid, "missionary work," and so forth. Increasingly important are Latin Americans coming to the United States, for a weekend of shopping in Miami or a year of washing dishes in Chicago or four years in New Haven for a doctorate in economics. Visitors to the United States return with, among other things, social status, especially if they return with an advanced degree. Indeed, a graduate degree from a good United States university has become almost a prerequisite for being a cabinet minister in Latin America, and it does not hurt, either, for serving in the highest public office—the presidency.

The former Mexican president Ernesto Zedillo grew up in Mexicali, on the border with California. His ticket to the presidency: a doctorate in economics from Yale University. (Zedillo's successor, Vicente Fox, had a different kind of "socialization": his stint working with the United States–based "multinational" company, Coca-Cola.) The Costa Rican president, Miguel Angel Rodríguez, has a doctorate in economics from the University of California, Berkeley. Most illustrative, though, is the former president of Bolivia, Gonzalo Sánchez de Lozada, given in Bolivia the nickname El Gringo.

Gonzalo Sánchez de Lozada, the son of an exiled Bolivian diplomat, grew up in the United States. After finishing his study of philosophy at the University of Chicago, Sánchez de Lozada settled in Bolivia, where he made a fortune in mining. Next came politics. He was appointed to serve as planning minister in 1986, and from that position he pushed privatization of state assets and services. Sánchez de Lozada resigned in 1988 to begin his campaign for the 1989 presidential elections. He won the most votes in the elections but did not become president, because of Bolivia's complex electoral system. Four years later he enlisted United States political consultants and used opinion polls to help formulate his stands on issues.

One of Sánchez de Lozada's opponents in the 1993 presidential elections boasted that he spoke Spanish well. Sánchez de Lozada is most comfortable speaking English; he speaks Spanish with a pronounced "American accent," giving rise to his nickname, El Gringo. Similarly, a fifty-centavo coin came to be called a "Goni," Sánchez de Lozada's other nickname, because of being *half* a boliviano. Yet, in his 1993 presidential campaign, Sánchez de Lozada's advisers sought to emphasize, rather than diminish, their candidate's accent in television spots because the image of *el gringo* produced confidence in Sánchez de Lozada's abilities and in his honesty.

El Gringo won the election. What he brought from the United States to the presidency of Bolivia, though, was much more than an accent. He brought a commitment to "free markets" and a concomitant dislike of "big government," of political centralization and of extensive state intervention in the economy. For someone raised in the United States, even someone far from being "conservative," Bolivia appeared to have gone overboard in vesting authority in the state, and the evidence appeared overwhelming that the Bolivian state was far from "efficient." In other words, Sánchez de Lozada stood out in Bolivia not just because he talked like a *gringo* but because he thought like a *gringo*. And given the prerogatives of the presidency, Sánchez de Lozada pushed through many economic and political reforms in Bolivia. For example, in addition to selling off state-owned monopolies, Sánchez de Lozada successfully pursued a political decentralization that steered government revenue to poor villages and municipalities.

By the end of his tenure, Sánchez de Losada's popularity had plummeted. But when I talked to him about his term, he shrugged off criticism and told me, "The task of a politician is to turn popularity into respect." And, in fact, Gonzalo Sánchez de Lozada is respected. He did much to "transform" Bolivia, changes that make the country, the poorest in South America, administratively more rational and, not incidentally, a little more like the United States. His upbringing and education in the United States surely shaped the kinds of changes Gonzalo Sánchez de Lozada pursued in Bolivia. So, perhaps, it is fitting that his nickname is El Gringo.

Speaking to Sánchez de Lozada, though, raises questions about just what is "nationalism" and how exclusive it should be. Sánchez de Lozada may be El Gringo, and he may have participated in politics with a sense of noblesse oblige that some found haughty, but he clearly cares deeply about Bolivia and as president did what he thought was best for the nation. And even Spratling, who could not even claim to be at least *half* a Mexican, is recognized by many Mexicans as having contributed to Mexico's culture—and so its national identity. Yet confusion continues. A non-Hispanic historian from the United States who has done careful archival work in Puerto Rico—which he has published—recounts how he once was accused on the island of "stealing Puerto Rico's history."

Throughout most of the twentieth century, Latin Americans have had a binary view of the United States (and, by extension, of Canada). The United States has represented both the admirably "successful" country to the north, and the arrogant hegemony that exploits the region. (Gringos thus have borne a confusing burden of allegory.) As the twentieth century came to a close, though, fears of imperialism, economic dependency, "Americanization," "dollarization," and "Disney-ization" eased. Instead, there is now talk of the inevitability of "globalization" and simple indifference.

The Brazilian intellectual Oswald de Andrade argued in the 1920s for a metaphorical "cannibalism" in Latin America. The proposal was to ingest everything foreign in order to forge a new synthesis that could be turned against the foreigner. Well, sometimes it seems in Latin America that everything foreign is, in fact, ingested. And something new is almost always created. Foreign—usually a euphemism for the United States—goods, techniques, and models mesh with local cultures that are pliant but not prostrate. Latin America is too voluminous and too entangled to be simply remade in the image of the United States. But where de Andrade and succeeding disaffected intellectuals erred was in expecting a collision with the United States. *El gringo*, with whatever he happens to be bringing, may be feted, copied, ridiculed, or fleeced, but he—or she—is still almost always welcome in Latin America. A persistent characterization of Latin America is that it is susceptible to the influence of the United States.

# Chapter 13

## What to Paint?

LATIN AMERICAN artists are often seen by their *paisanos* as embodiments of the national consciousness. The artist equals the nation; the sum of nations equals Latin America. This equation is a heavy—and unfair—burden for artists. The art of the region is vast and diverse. And despite shared cultural traits, each Latin American country has an "artistic personality" of its own. But still, what Latin American artists are up to surely does say something about their society, especially if the artist is rewarded with public acclaim.

Latin American art of the 1920s, the 1930s, and the 1940s was "stirred up" by the radical artistic developments that transformed the visual arts in Europe in the first decades of the twentieth century—fauvism, expressionism, cubism, Dada, purism, constructivism, and surrealism—and by sweeping political change—the Mexican Revolution, the Russian Revolution, the birth of the Spanish Republic, and the rise of fascism in Germany and Italy. European trends in the arts did not enter Latin America as intact or discrete styles, but instead were adapted in individual, uneven (but sometimes innovative), and idiosyncratic ways. Cataclysmic political events of the era, especially the Mexican Revolution, perhaps elicited a more uniform response, that of inciting a cultural nationalism.

The arts were redirected to reflect national pride and progress. This change was most notable in Mexico, so charged by its revolution, but other countries in the region followed suit. National values and symbols were portrayed in a "social realist" style. Prominent in the iconography were scenes of everyday life of the poor majority (both urban and rural). In countries with a significant indigenous population, such as Mexico and the Andean countries, indigenous life was celebrated. Images were often of a highly politicized nature. Depicted were both the iconography of progress (showing, for example, education programs) as well as that of the oppression of the poor. Most art of the era was socially committed.

Some of the art of the period, though, was less ideologically charged. At times art was just picturesque, contributing to—especially abroad—a folkloric image of the region. And at least a few artists, including the celebrated Frida Kahlo, explored the labyrinths of their psyche. But, again, most art of the era was socially committed, reflecting the political tenor of the times and a sense of social responsibility among many of the most talented artists. Art of this era was accessible and remains familiar.

Paradoxically, Latin America's most renowned artists from this nationalist era, those who are held to have best represented the culture of the region, had strong ties to Europe. Mexico's famed muralist painter Diego Rivera spent the whole period of the Mexican Revolution in Europe, much of it in Paris. The counterpart to the painting of murals was printmaking. But Mexican graphic artists, such as Leopoldo Méndez, were introduced to woodcuts by Jean Charlot, who arrived from France in 1921. Charlot also appears to have disseminated the work of German expressionists and revived interest in the work of the Mexican graphic artist José Guadalupe Posada. Latin American "constructivist" art can be traced to the Uruguayan artist Joaquín Torres-García, who returned to Montevideo in 1934 after forty years in Europe and the United States. Brazil's two celebrated "modernists" also were linked to Europe. Tarsila do Amaral studied in Paris, where she frequented the studio of Fernand Léger. Lazar Segall was born in Russia, and trained in Berlin and Dresden. He arrived in Brazil in 1913, returned to Europe, but settled permanently in São Paulo in 1923. Segall introduced German expressionism to Brazilian artists. From Europe, too, came surrealism. One of Latin America's two renowned "surrealists" was the Cuban Wifredo Lam. He spent nearly his entire adult life in Europe. The other noted surrealist is the Chilean Roberto Matta. He has also lived almost exclusively in Europe.

European-trained artists, and European artists who immigrated to Latin America, embraced local cultures from which they were quite distant socially. The same holds for the artists who either worked in New York or were from the United States. Some of the most picturesque renderings of peasant life in Mexico are from Miguel Covarrubias, a natty artist who worked for a while in New York illustrating the magazine *Vanity Fair*. Covarrubias and similar socially situated artists, in fact, spawned *indigenismo*, the sympathetic portrayal of indigenous people. Likewise, although these artists tended to live deep within large cities, they often painted lush fauna from faraway jungles; and although they were overwhelmingly of European extraction, they often had a deep interest in pre-Columbian artifacts and cultures. Dawn Ades, in a survey of Latin American art, notes:

> The Brazilian *modernistas* in the 1920s were an elite and privileged group, living a cosmopolitan life and traveling freely to Europe. . . . A critic later remarked on the spectacle of Tarsila, returning from Paris with her Poiret dresses, to teach the people how to be Brazilian.

And there is the irony of Torres-García who, after spending most of his own life abroad, wrote a manifesto arguing:

> I believe the age of colonialism and importation is past (now I am talking primarily about what we call culture), so away with whoever speaks, in literary terms, a language other than our own natural language (I do not say criollo), be they writers, painters, or composers! If

they did not learn the lessons of Europe when they should have done, too bad for them because the moment has passed.

If nothing else, Torres-García, writing his manifesto in 1935, was premature in dismissing the siren of Europe and the United States.

The end of the Second World War brought with it a dramatic change in the artistic climate of Latin America. Artists looked beyond their indigenous subject matter, prompted in part by the growing dominance of the New York school of abstract expressionism. New York became the new mecca. Although abstraction remains popular, many artists have returned to figurative art, but often in a much-transformed way. The influence of surrealism and expressionism lingers.

Though there has been greater plurality in the second half of the twentieth century, Latin American art has become decidedly less nationalistic and less socially committed. Regardless of the "style" of presentation, it has become more academic, more cerebral, and more tied to the psyche of the artist. For example, the work of the Mexican artist Nahum Zenil, who has received considerable attention, explores his personal anxieties of being a homosexual in the traditional social framework of Mexico. The art historian Edward Sullivan describes the common denominators of Zenil's work as being "self-absorption, self-possession, and narcissism." Similarly, the Venezuelan artist Alexander Apóstol makes creative use of photography to explore the "enigma of identity."

The caprices and challenges of being a Latin American artist at the juncture of the twentieth and twenty-first centuries are suggested by a Brazilian artist, Marcia Grostein. Marcia is a successful artist, but she is not a prominent artist. But which Latin American artist born in the aftermath of the Second World War, and so truly an artist of the second half of the twentieth century, is prominent? The 1997 fall and spring sales of Latin American art by the auction house Sotheby's are revealing. Only 14 percent of the artists whose work was offered were born after the Second World War. And none of the contemporary artists represented in Sotheby's auctions is well known. There are so many young (and middle-aged) Latin American artists. But their art has not seized the public imagination, even of that small segment in Latin America who are university educated.

Marcia is the daughter of Jewish emigrants to Brazil. Her mother came from Russia and her father from Poland. Family lore has it that a paternal ancestor was one of Napoleon's financiers. But the turmoil of Europe drove both sides of Marcia's family to South America. Marcia's extended family is spread throughout southern Brazil, Uruguay, and Argentina. Her own family settled in São Paulo, where her father opened a jewelry store. Marcia's mother saw to it that Marcia had a good education, one steeped in European culture. Marcia had piano lessons and studied ballet. And Marcia was frequently taken to see an aunt who was an artist. The aunt taught Marcia to draw. Marcia remembers being taken with the work of the Italian artist Amedeo Modigliani and spending hours copying his portraits. But dancing was her passion. Her father, though, firmly said, "My daughter is not just going to be a dancer."

So art it was. In 1969, at the age of nineteen, Marcia went to London to study drawing and painting (above all with watercolors) at the Royal Academy of Art. She recalls being drawn to the watercolors of the famed nineteenth-century English painter J.M.W. Turner. She spent hours looking at his work in the Tate Gallery.

After two years in London, Marcia returned to Brazil in 1970. Brazil was in turmoil. The armed forces were clumsily repressing small groups trying to ignite a socialist revolution. Neighboring Uruguay and Argentina were in even more turmoil. But Marcia was not drawn to politics. She remained focused on art. And, as she says, "At the time, art did not mean much in Brazil." The country's folk art did not "touch" her, and neither did the country's colonial or "modern" artists. Yet Marcia continued to draw and to paint. Icons for her were the English painter Francis Bacon and the American—or New York—painter Willem de Kooning. In 1977, at age twenty-eight, Marcia left Brazil, moving to New York.

One summer day on one of Long Island's nicer beaches, Marcia was introduced to "the assistant" of Willem de Kooning. Marcia could not resist asking for de Kooning's telephone number and calling him, saying, "My dream is to meet you. Is that possible?" They met the next day, at ten in the morning. She stayed until eleven that night. Another day she showed him photographs of her work, asking him not to critique the work, but instead to recommend a teacher. He said, "You don't need a teacher; you need to show your work in New York." De Kooning introduced her first New York exhibit, giving her a breach into the vaunted world of "established artists."

Other shows followed, in both museums and galleries. And Marcia's work has been included with the work of other contemporary artists in museum exhibits. Public showings of her work have enabled her to sell paintings and, more recently, sculpture. In many though not all showings of her work, Marcia is identified as a Brazilian artist. For example, her work was included in a 1985 exhibit titled "Today's Art of Brazil," at the Hara Museum of Contemporary Art in Tokyo. In 1994 her work was included in an exhibit titled "Small Formats in Latin America," at a gallery in Puerto Rico. Moreover, in her native Brazil her work has not only been shown in private galleries, but also included in the biennials of São Paulo. Thus, in Brazil she is accepted as a "Brazilian artist." Indeed, she has been honored with a twenty-year retrospective at the Museu de Arte de São Paulo and the Museu de Arte Moderna do Rio de Janeiro.

Marcia is aware of the different facets of her identity: a Brazilian, a member of a large but tight-knit family with a European heritage, a Jew, a woman, a New Yorker, an artist. . . . But Marcia says she has no special affinity for any one facet of her identity. She does not want to be part of any clique or part of any movement. She dislikes labels. She draws a parallel with how she clothes herself: she aspires "to have style, but not to follow fashion." When I, daringly, asked her what makes her art "Brazilian," she replied, after a shrug of her shoulders, that her work "reflects the color, energy, and anxiety of Brazil."

An erudite art historian in New York, trained at Columbia University and specializing in medieval European art, gave me a cruel but haunting critique of Latin American art. He said it is *derivative*, the dreaded word in art criticism, suggesting there is little that is original. Latin American art, he said, is not much more than René Magritte— French surrealism—Ernst Kirchner—German expressionism—and assorted tropical motifs. I asked Marcia what she thought of the caustic remark. I was surprised when she said, "Oh, I agree."

For Marcia, though, it is now New York that has a hold over Latin American artists. "To be a successful Latin American artist, you have to come through New York. Doing so—and prospering—gives you the stamp of approval, which is foolish, but that is the way it is." Marcia adds, however, "It is dangerous coming to New York. You lose your purity."

Marcia has prospered in New York. After being introduced by de Kooning at the Suydan Gallery, she had a solo exhibit at the Sutton Gallery. A blurb for that exhibit was written by the artist James Rosenquist, with whom she had a relationship. He was, Marcia acknowledges, helpful to her career. And Marcia met Betty Parsons, a celebrated art dealer, fond of promoting "new talent." She showed Marcia's work. Subsequently, Marcia had a relationship with another celebrated New York–based artist, Malcolm Morley. They were together five years, part of which—sandwiched in the middle—they were married (the only time Marcia says she has been "married on paper"). Marcia always wanted to have children, but it never came to be. But Marcia is comfortable in New York. She has a wealth of friends and "contacts," a beautiful apartment between Madison Avenue and Park Avenue (on the Upper East Side), and her cherished walks in Central Park.

In New York, Marcia works in the living room of her apartment.

(In São Paulo she has a studio.) Marcia does not have a routine for working. And she does not have a plan for how much time she spends in New York and how much time she stays in Brazil. She can go three months without working, though during this time she may, as she says, promote her work, look for opportunities to exhibit it, and sell it. When Marcia turns to creating art, she often works all day and well into the night for weeks on end. If she is painting, she goes straight to a blank canvas; she does not do preliminary sketches. She takes a long time to finish a composition—repainting and repainting until she is satisfied. She also does sculpture—especially of chairs—and sometimes "chore-ography," which is photographed, recording a series of images. Marcia says her art is influenced by everything. She strives to avoid what she feels is a common fault of artists—to find a formula and never evolve. If there is a constant to Marcia's art, across mediums, it is, she believes, that all her art "has some ironic content."

One of Marcia's most well-received paintings, one that has been exhibited on numerous occasions, is a large work titled *Matisse in the Ocean and Crabs in the Sky*. The painting is a riot of creatures from a tidal pool, thrown together and rendered in bright colors—red, yellow, orange, green, blue, and violet. I like the painting. It conveys energy, unease, and all the mystery of the sea. As I looked at the painting in Marcia's apartment, she explained to me that she conceived the work when Mikhail Gorbachev was visiting the United States. Marcia thought of Henri Matisse's two paintings called *Dance*, one copy of which is in Russia (then the Soviet Union) and the other in the United States (at the Museum of Modern Art in New York).

In addition to painting, Marcia produces sculpture, most of which are renderings of chairs. Why chairs? Marcia explains that she herself did not know for some time. But through "therapy," she concluded that she was haunted by the memory of her mother, who was reduced to sitting in a chair, watching "soap operas" on television, after learning that her husband—Marcia's father—was having an affair with one of her friends. Seeing her mother wasting away hurt Marcia; it depressed her. Marcia's chairs are sometimes small, sometimes large, always dis-torted—or contorted. While in Brazil in early 1999, Marcia created two works of art that I find engaging. One work is titled *Political Stress*. It is the frame of a beach chair, which has been "wrapped" with newspaper clippings of articles on politics. The second work is titled *Cultural Stress*. It is another beach chair, stripped to its frame, which has been plastered with newspaper articles about cultural events. *Cultural Stress*, Marcia explains, refers to all of the fervor in Brazil to see cultural events that actually have no depth, that are attended just for the oppor-tunity "to be seen" by members of one's social class—or, better yet, to be seen and noticed by members of a higher social class. At the same time, Marcia says, in Brazil there can be a wonderful play that no one will attend because it is being performed in the middle of "nowhere."

I liked the two works, but I quickly realized that without the presence of Marcia to explain what had prompted her to create the two works, I would not pay attention to them. In fact, walking by them—if they were in a museum—I might even disparage them. Like much contemporary Latin American art, Marcia's art is cerebral, and so—to the casual viewer—much of the art is inaccessible. Part of the "art" is the concept that inspired it, the context in which it was produced, and the life of the artist. But most viewers—real or potential—do not have the opportunity to do more than glance at the "plastic art" and, perhaps, read from a small label what is often an enigmatic title.

Similarly, in an interview in the winter 2000 issue of the magazine *Bomb*, another Brazilian sculptor, Ernesto Neto, described his work in baffling terms:

> My work is first and foremost a contemporary sculpture, it speaks of the finite and the infinite, of the macroscopic and the microscopic, the internal and the external, by the masculine and feminine powers, but sex is like a snake, it slithers through everything.

What, exactly, does this description tell us? I am not sure. But Ernesto Neto, too, like Marcia, is "successful."

Marcia's art is in museum and private collections in Latin America (Brazil, Uruguay, and Argentina), the United States, Europe, and Japan. The acquisition of her work delights Marcia. She is proudest of the purchase of one of her paintings by the Metropolitan Museum of Art in New York. The piece is an oil painting titled *The Sacred Garden of Adam*. The work is part of a series of paintings Marcia did from 1988 to 1990 of imaginary gardens. The subject of the painting is a lone monkey perched on a rococo-looking branch. Behind the monkey is an off-blue sky; on either side is vegetation adorned with flowers. The painting is thick with paint, the monkey and his roost rendered in an expressionistic style.

Marcia says that although the Metropolitan Museum of Art had previously been given works of art by Brazilians, her painting was the first by a Brazilian to have been purchased by the venerable museum. The painting is not on permanent exhibition, but Marcia believes it has been twice put out for exhibition in the galleries of twentieth-century art. I do not know what prompted curators to select the painting for purchase (which they did through a gallery). But I can not help but feel that the painting and its purchase by the Metropolitan Museum is ironic. Whatever else the painting is, it is a picture of a monkey in the jungle. This image surely can be seen in Brazil; the Amazon is certainly full of monkeys in trees. But is this the image of Brazil, a country of 160 million people and the world's tenth largest economy, to be seen in New York, in a gallery dedicated to the work of the twentieth century? And does it take a Brazilian of Marcia's background, training, and talent to contribute such a "picturesque" or "folkloric" image of such a large and complex country? Or am I a prisoner of my long-held association of Latin American art with the murals of Diego Rivera, overflowing with their piercing social commentary and political idealism?

Marcia is proud of her art and enjoys creating it. There are other artists whose company she courts and artists whose work she admires. Among her fellow Latin Americans, for example, she likes the work of the Cuban artist José Bedia (who resides in Miami). And Marcia admires contemporary Latin American photography. Still, Marcia is disenchanted with "the art world." Being an artist, she says, is difficult. There are so many artists and such competition. Success can be so transient; you can be passed through a corridor of fame "like a potato." Artists have "to hype themselves, do the politics" to find a livable place in a cruel hierarchy, "where if I am someone powerful, I can make you a star in two minutes." (Left unsaid, I suppose, is that if I am powerful, I can also take your stardom away if I want.) What is slighted in this "marketing" is the art itself. Moreover, according to Marcia, artists are increasingly atomized. Yes, there are art journals that serve as forums, but true community among artists is rare. Marcia is creative, energetic, and savvy, but she is still hostage of the caprices and constraints of the "art world."

At the juncture of the twentieth and twenty-first centuries, the sensibilities, the aspirations, and even—perhaps—the art of Latin American artists seem prescribed by a larger social context, one that is anxious to be free of unsettling political questions, international (or "global") in setting standards and tastes, rushed, atomized, self-conscious, and unabashedly elitist.

# Chapter 14

## Migration

### Horizontales

1. Perteneciente a varón
6. Perteneciente a varón
9. Perteneciente a varón
10. Perteneciente a varón
11. Perteneciente a varón
13. Perteneciente a varón
14. Perteneciente a varón
17. Perteneciente a varón
18. Perteneciente a varón
19. Perteneciente a varón
20. Perteneciente a varón
21. Perteneciente a varón
75. Perteneciente a varón
76. Perteneciente a varón

### Verticales

1. Perteneciente a varón
2. Perteneciente a varón
3. Perteneciente a varón
4. Perteneciente a varón
5. Perteneciente a varón
6. Perteneciente a varón
7. Perteneciente a varón
8. Perteneciente a varón
53. Perteneciente a varón
54. Perteneciente a varón
55. Perteneciente a varón
60. Perteneciente a varón
61. Perteneciente a varón

IN EARLY 1999, Gonzalo returned to his native Chile. He had not been home for so long and the trip from New York was so far, and so expensive, that he went for a month. But after only two weeks, Gonzalo was ready to come "home"—back to the world he had made for himself in Oyster Bay, Long Island, New York, United States of America. Upon his return to Oyster Bay, he decided to change his citizenship—that would be how he would mark the "millennium," the passing to the year 2000.

Gonzalo came to Oyster Bay, a wealthy community on Long Island Sound, an hour and a half outside of New York City, in 1987, at the urging of his sister Carmen. She had come two years before at the prompting of a friend, a fellow Chilean. Gonzalo took care of an elderly widow. After she passed away, he began to work for others in the neighborhood, working as a "handyman" and "caretaker." He worked hard to learn English, took courses to receive his high school equivalency certificate, got a driver's license, and bought a secondhand car. His first drive into New York City, on his own, in his own car, gave him a tremendous feeling of accomplishment and of pride.

Gonzalo left Chile because of a sense that the country offered him few opportunities. He is the last of ten children, born of poor farmers living south of Chile's capital, Santiago. Gonzalo was born in 1957; he was thus only thirteen when Salvador Allende, with his "democratic road to socialism," assumed the presidency of Chile. Still, Gonzalo remembers the tumultuous period. His memory is not of imminent liberation, but of chaos and anarchy, of needless confrontation and violence. An especially poignant memory is the thrashing of merchandise in stores whose owners elected not to support Allende's "popular unity" struggle for revolutionary change. Allende's efforts at revamping Chile were made in the name of poor Chileans like Gonzalo and his family. However, Gonzalo embraced the military regime of Augusto Pinochet that seized power in 1973 with a bloody coup d'état. The military was relentless in repressing the Communist and Socialist parties, as well as labor unions and other groups that had supported or taken part in the Allende regime. About three thousand people were executed or "disappeared," and tens of thousands more were jailed (and sometimes tortured) or forced into exile. At the head of the military, and so of the government, was Pinochet, who was to become a towering figure, governing Chile for seventeen years—until 1990. For many Chileans, Pinochet was evil. For other Chileans, including Gonzalo, Pinochet was a savior, restoring order and ushering in an era of prosperity for Chile.

The irony is that although Gonzalo has always supported Pinochet, the Chile Pinochet created—based on liberal economic doctrine—offered no room for Gonzalo, and he ended up deciding that it was best to abandon his country. Macroeconomic indicators suggest Chile prospered under Pinochet's rule, and that it continues to prosper now that Chile is guided not just by liberal economic institutions and practices, but governed, too, by a liberal democracy. But for Gonzalo, bouncing between rural Chile and Santiago, remunerative employment was always elusive.

Gonzalo came to the United States in 1987 at the age of thirty. The transition was difficult. The word he uses for those first few years is a word seemingly hard for him to utter, as if the mere thought of it brings back a flood of sad memories: lonely. But now, after so many years in Oyster Bay, Gonzalo is comfortable, at home. His sister Carmen is still in Oyster Bay, and Chileans have followed Chileans: Oyster Bay now has many Chileans, who in a quiet way meet many of the mundane needs of the community. They are all but invisible except to each other. Their own modest needs—as Chileans—are met by phone cards, the post office, and the International Deli & Grocery, a tiny shop in front of a grand building that once served as the summer offices of Theodore Roosevelt (whose summer residence was nearby Sagamore Hill). Gonzalo is one of the Chileans who has persuaded the Dominican owner of the International Deli to stock Chilean products, including the soft drinks Pap and Bilz, Super 8 chocolate bars, canned *mote con huesillos* (a sweet confection of apricots and corn), and Chilean newspapers (which cost $4.50 each).

In Oyster Bay there are many Salvadorans, too. And in a neighboring town there is a colony of Peruvians. Gonzalo respects *"americanos,"* as he calls non-Hispanic, *white* citizens of the United States. (African-Americans are referred to separately, but without malice, as *"negros"* [blacks]; Asian-Americans are likewise referred to separately, and also without malice, as *"chinos"* [Chinese].) However, Gonzalo's friends are other *"hispanos,"* with whom he feels he shares three central traits: immigrant status, Spanish, and soccer. Not all of Gonzalo's friends are Chilean, but he feels closest to Chileans, and he is generally wary of Salvadorans, whom he finds rowdy. Gonzalo and Carmen stay in touch with their family in Chile, especially their aging parents, to whom they send money on a regular basis. And they give advice, too, via telephone, in what sometimes seems like life via "remote control."

Gonzalo is far from being alone in his migration from Latin America to the United States. In the second half of the twentieth century, there has been an extraordinary movement of peoples from Latin America to the United States. The movement is extraordinary in part because of the sheer number of people involved. There have always been people of Hispanic descent in the United States, especially after 1848, when Mexico was forced to cede more than half of its territory to the United States, what is now the "Southwest" of the United States. Suddenly, many Mexicans became "foreigners in their own land." But recent migration has vastly augmented the population in the United States of what Gonzalo calls *hispanos*.

It is difficult to measure just how much the Hispanic population has grown since 1776, 1848, 1900, 1950, or any other date before 1980. The 1980 census was the first careful attempt to count persons of Hispanic origin, a count that totaled 14 million. Between 1980 and 2000, the Hispanic population grew at an astonishing rate—to 35 million, representing 12 percent of the population of the United States. The total Hispanic population of the United States is larger than the entire population of Canada, and growing five times faster than the rest of the population of the United States.

This movement of people is also extraordinary because it is simply the result of millions of individual (and family) decisions. The United States as a nation-state never discussed, debated, or decided to change so fundamentally its population, its society. Likewise, no nation-state in Latin America planned or decided to divide and separate its society so wrenchingly, with up to 20 percent—in the case of El Salvador—leaving within a brief span of time. But migration has irrevocably changed the United States and Latin America, as well as the lives of the millions who have moved.

How Hispanics in the United States fare is an important question, and one with many consequences for Latin America. One issue will be identity: the term Hispanic puts millions of people from a variety of national backgrounds into a single "ethnic" category with no allowance for their differences in class, race, gender, and length of residence in the United States. Will a "pan-Hispanic identity" emerge, or will divisions, such as of national background, be salient? Will migrants from Latin America prosper? Will they assimilate, or will they retain in large measure their cultural identity (which seemingly would facilitate continuing ties to Latin America)?

It is too early to answer these questions with any certainty. Newly arrived Hispanic immigrants often start at the "bottom" of the economy, finding only poorly paid employment. Indeed, an estimated 40 percent of Hispanic children in the United States live in poverty. But millions of Hispanics are also moving into the middle class. And some Hispanics have truly prospered. The most generous patron of the Metropolitan Opera in New York is a Cuban immigrant, Alberto Vilar, who, among his many donations to the Metropolitan Opera, has given $25 million to the endowment fund, money he made in "high-tech" investing. (The "grand tier" of the Metropolitan Opera "house" has been renamed the Vilar Grand Tier.) At a luncheon of the Metropolitan Opera Guild, I asked Vilar if he receives requests to help the Hispanic community: "All the time." "What do you say?" "I pay my taxes." Vilar is apparently interested in opera and not much else. In the decades to come, how many Hispanics will remain mired in poverty, how many will move into the middle class, and how many—like Vilar—will attain positions of leadership and wealth (and what will they do with their resources)? And what will be the impact on the established Hispanic community of the constant arrival of more Latin Americans to the United States?

There is a budding group of intellectuals, many sheltered in universities, that speak for the Hispanic community in a militant, urgent voice. But most Hispanics, including Gonzalo out in Long Island, are quite traditional: family-centered, religious, hardworking, and respectful. It is not clear who speaks for them or, more important, what kind of decisions they will make in the twenty-first century. It also remains to be seen how different ethnic groups in the United States, and the institutions of the country, will accommodate the growing presence of Hispanics.

Within Latin America, too, there are many yet to be answered questions about the impact of such widescale immigration. To date, most immigration from Latin America to the United States has been from Mexico (nearly two-thirds of Hispanics in the United States are Mexican-American), the Caribbean, and Central America—those parts of Latin America closest to the United States. However, migration to the United States from South America has been growing rapidly, especially from Colombia and Ecuador. All Latin American countries have a "community" in the United States, and there is considerable travel back and forth between each country and the United States. As the United States comes to have a larger Hispanic population, and with so many Latin Americans visiting, too, Latin America has enhanced—and easier—access to the United States and its offerings, including its culture.

The most immediate impact, though, of migration is conceptualized as being country-specific: the amount of money sent home by migrants—*remesas*—and the impact the money has on the country's economy, especially its balance of payments. In the small countries of the Caribbean and Central America, *remesas* have come to be a significant source of foreign exchange. El Salvador receives well over $1 billion a year sent home by its sons and daughters who have migrated, seven times more than the country earns from its most important export, coffee. The economy of El Salvador is sustained in large measure by *remesas*. The same can be said of Nicaragua, the Dominican Republic, and—now, ironically—Cuba. In Mexico, and in Guatemala, too, *remesas* support many marginal regions and assist the national economy by providing the foreign exchange needed to maintain exports. Will the checks continue, or will a Guatemalan banker be prescient: "In a generation no one is even going to remember us"?

Migration does diffuse culture. Migrants, especially those who go back and forth between the United States and Latin America, disseminate, often unknowingly, culture. And the diffusion of culture is not necessarily just a matter of sharing purchases from a local mall and personal habits; there may be a significant freight of beliefs and values. Peter Berger argues, for example, that a compact disk of music also may symbolize self-expression, spontaneity, released sexuality, and defiance of tradition and authority. Given the size, wealth, and prominence of the United States, the diffusion of culture is asymmetrical. Writing in the fall 1997 issue of *National Interest*, Berger argues:

> Mexicans eat *hamburguesas*, Americans eat tacos. But the Mexicans are consuming whole chunks of American values "in, with, and under" the American hamburgers; the Americans are certainly *not* absorbing nonculinary aspects of Mexican culture by eating tacos.

Some disagree, confident that Latin Americans—or Latinos here in the United States—can retain their cultural identity regardless of what they consume. Still others argue that Berger is right, but that retreat into a cultural hermeticism is impossible, and that, in any case, Latin America was created by just such collisions between cultures. Why stop now? These are potent issues, still being debated.

While the United States is the most frequent destination for Latin Americans who leave their country (99 percent of Mexicans who live outside of Mexico live in the United States), there are other destinations, usually neighboring countries. One out of ten in Costa Rica is Nicaraguan, and given differences in "fertility," one out of five births in Costa Rica is to Nicaraguan parents. Colombians migrate to Venezuela. Peruvians move to Chile. Bolivians move to Argentina. Brazilians move to Paraguay. Dominicans move to Puerto Rico. There are even Brazilians of Japanese descent returning—for good—to the country of their grandparents. And, within the countries of Latin America, there is much movement, from one region to another or from rural areas to cities. Latin America is a region of considerable dislocation.

In a stirring essay titled (translated into English), "A Country that Bleeds Itself," published in the August 5–11, 1999, issue of *El Seminario*, the noted writer Sergio Ramírez laments migration in his native Nicaragua and fixes the blame on the inability of the nation to respond to the needs of its people. What he says can be generalized, perhaps, for Latin America at large:

> Nicaragua is exporting its human potential. It is exporting itself. This exodus without parallel is even larger than that caused by the war of

the 1980s, and even more catastrophic because its causes are economic: unemployment, poverty without hope. Nicaraguans leave . . .
to search for what they cannot find in their own country: work, hope
for the future, and security for their families. . . . I see the desertion of
Nicaraguans as a great failure on our part. . . . water flows out of a
broken gutter.

Ramírez appears to write with as much sadness as anger. But he is
seething when he writes, for example, "Nicaraguans are helping other
countries grow and develop, but Nicaragua is becoming a mutilated
country."

The story of migration in Latin America, including migration out of
the region, to the United States, is one of endless individual frustrations,
challenges, and—if all goes well—renewed hope. But the story also has
a political dimension, one that is undeservedly obscured. Political con-
formity is a result of having the disaffected, the ambitious, migrate. For
political elites, this migration is a "relief." Individual "exit strategies,"
as a common solution to grave problems, serve as a political and economic "safety valve" for regimes that might otherwise be overwhelmed
by demands for radical change.

Gonzalo would say, though, that radical change would only be dis-
ruptive, forcing still more to flee. Gonzalo is looking forward to buying
a new car.

# Chapter 15

## Conclusion

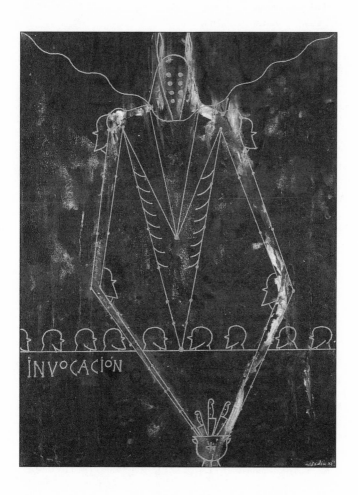

IN MARCH 1999 the Inter-American Development Bank, with the financial support of the Swedish government, offered a seminar titled "Latin America on the Eve of a New Century: The Vision of the New Generation." One hundred Latin Americans were invited, all judged to be "leaders" in their respective professions and all less than forty years old. Those in the group included political leaders (ministers and members of congress), writers, journalists, academics, directors of nongovernmental organizations, and successful business executives and entrepreneurs. The two-day seminar was held in Paris, at the offices of the United Nations Educational, Scientific, and Cultural Organization (UNESCO). Among those addressing the group were the Colombian novelist Gabriel García Márquez and the Guatemalan human-rights activist Rigoberta Menchú. Participants divided themselves into four groups to discuss their views of the future of Latin America.

In June 1999 a subset of the group—thirty-two young Latin Americans—met for a second seminar, held at the campus of INCAE in Costa Rica. I was invited to lead a workshop that would help participants articulate their vision of what kind of Latin America they wanted in the future. The group could hardly be judged to be a representative sample of Latin Americans. Nonetheless, those present were an extraordinarily talented group of young Latin Americans. What they had to say was surprising, captivating, and inspiring.

For the purpose of our workshop, participants were again divided into four groups. Four topics were selected to ground the discussions, which we hoped would lead to the conceptualization of a desirable vision of Latin America in the future. The topics were: (1) economics, (2) society, (3) relationship with the rest of the world, and (4) politics. Each of the four groups was assigned a topic. I briefly suggested a set of issues for each topic, but emphasized that the issues I had selected were meant only to stimulate their thinking, that each group should define for itself what it wished to discuss. We adjourned to small rooms, and the discussions began. The understanding was that after an hour and a half or so we would reconvene and listen to presentations from each group.

After everyone was settled, I slipped into the room of group three. The discussion was frank and lively. The question was posed as to how Latin America was perceived outside the region. The answers were not gratifying: "poor," "cheap labor," "not so interesting," "a source of migrants," "a source of *unwanted* migrants," "a bridge for drug traffic," and a "political—but not an economic—ally." I sensed that these were their perceptions of how Latin America was viewed from the United States: the world outside of Latin America was conflated into the United States. There was no rancor expressed toward the United

States. And no one said that the unflattering perceptions of Latin America were without foundation. Instead, the group moved to discuss how Latin Americans needed to improve their own perception of themselves. Someone asked, "How can Latin Americans expect others to think well of us when we do not hold ourselves in esteem?"

A paradox was suggested: abroad, Latin Americans are nationalistic, proud of who they are and of where they have come from; but in Latin America itself there is—commonly—cynicism and stinging criticism of political institutions, the economy, and of society. The image was offered of the Mexican who left Mexico out of despair but who today lives in the United States with a Mexican flag above his bed. A member of the group from El Salvador recounted how at a meeting in El Salvador a fellow *paisano* declared, "I moved to the United States because I could not dream in El Salvador. There are no opportunities here."

The emigration of so many fellow Latin Americans was held to be understandable but still a loss *and* a damning indictment of the region. Latin Americans needed, it was argued, not a higher standard of living, but instead the ability to dream—to have confidence in their societies and in their institutions—and to have opportunities. The sentiment expressed was: let the *gringos* think whatever they wish of us, but let us work to think better of ourselves, of our society, of our respective countries, of our corner of the world. One key to success was judged to be better and more accessible education, which would provide greater equality of opportunity. A second necessity was held to be political and economic institutions—prominently governmental—that have public credibility.

After a while I got up and went to check on the other groups, all of which were having spirited discussions. In fact, when the appointed time came to regroup, it proved hard to entice participants to reconvene in the lecture hall. Once we were back together and listening to the presentations, summarizing the conversations of each group, I was struck by parallels with what I had heard in group three. First, there was a common language and a remarkable uniformity in how issues were analyzed. Second, there was no visible ideology. Third, there was a repeated call for unity, for an alliance between the state and the private sector, and—more broadly—for a search for consensus throughout society to solve problems and to develop an agenda for the future. Fourth, there was a sense of taking responsibility for the fate of the region and a resiliency. Fifth, and most surprising to me, there was a persistent call for a change in attitudes and in values. What Latin America needs more than anything else, they said, is not a transfusion of resources to the region, a redistribution of income and wealth, or any other kind of *material* remedy to the ills of the region. Instead, a change in culture is judged to be most necessary. Latin Americans need to have more faith in themselves, more pride, and to participate more actively and with more enthusiasm in the construction of a better society. The private sector needs to be more socially responsible. Democracy needs to be strengthened by a "new political culture," one that emphasizes participation, transparency, accountability, and credibility.

The group's expectation for Latin America's economy was sustained economic growth, but growth that offers "opportunities," including—above all—more and better employment. Economic growth should facilitate enhanced investments in education and health, in "human capital," and should be, moreover, environmentally sustainable. The private sector was held to be, necessarily, the "motor of development." However, the aspiration was that the region's private sector would be not just economically competitive, but also supportive of education and human development, and "transparent" in its activities. The state was assigned an economic role, that of promoting and facilitating productivity and competitiveness. And, again, there was a desire for the state to invest not just in infrastructure but in the poor, providing them with the wherewithal and means to participate productively in the economy. Public administration needs to be transparent and responsive to public needs.

What stood out in the discussion was the desire not for the highest possible rate of economic growth, but instead for an economy that would help the poor, not with handouts or with a violent redistribution of wealth, but instead through the creation of opportunity. There are two main paths to opportunity: (1) investment in education and other social services, and (2) eliminating favoritism and corruption.

The second presentation, on the *kind* of society desired in the future, echoed the presentation on hopes for the economy. The opening statement was: "We want a Latin American society with equality of opportunity for everyone, and everyone tolerant and respecting human dignity." Problems that need to be resolved include most prominently: inequality, poverty, and violence (political, criminal, and "domestic"). Again, education was judged to be instrumental in reshaping society. Education has to include the teaching of desired "values" to strengthen the "culture" that serves as a foundation to society.

The presentation on the relationship between Latin America and the rest of the world began with a discussion of "self-esteem." An argument was made, which appeared to be accepted by all present, that throughout Latin America there is a "lack of faith, confidence, and hope." The political and economic institutions of the region were deemed weak and so incapable of resolving problems. A contrast was drawn with the United States, where it was said—in English, ironically paraphrasing Martin Luther King—it is possible to claim, "I have a dream."

Seeds of change for a better future were perceived to be the end of ideological conflicts, many of them violent, within the region, efforts in many countries at "national dialogues," disparate "social movements," and a spurt of efforts at regional cooperation. Also arguing for an improved future is the sheer resiliency of Latin Americans, their success in having survived military regimes—and repression—economic chaos and crisis, ideological battles, and inept civilian governments. Those present in the seminar were, as it was said, "children of *la crisis*." They were young, anything but naïve, and energetic. And in their youth the group was representative: at the passing of the twentieth century—and the beginning of the twenty-first century—half of all Latin Americans are under the age of twenty-five. There is youth and there is vigor in Latin America.

The final presentation addressed politics. The opening statement of the group echoed the previous presentations. The thesis of the group was a call to "*profundizar la democracia a través de la creación de una nueva cultura política.*" Sloth, indifference, and corruption need to be combated. Political parties need to be truly representative and accountable to their constituents, political participation has to be cultivated, and the institutions of democracy—and the rule of law—strengthened. Ways of building national and regional consensus have to be found.

How striking it was to see representatives of so many countries speak in such harmony. But what was I hearing? Were the young Latin Americans critiquing the model of liberalism or its imperfect landing in the southern latitudes of the Americas? Or, were the participants in the seminar just looking to perfect—or to humanize—what was at hand, much like earlier calls in another part of the world for "socialism with a human face?"

I could not gauge the depth of their disappointment with the prevailing institutions of liberalism, with the prosaic workings of democracy and capitalism in their respective countries. The thinking, the reflections, of the group were certainly shaped by the absence of any perceived alternative to democracy and capitalism. One cannot categorically reject a model unless there is a ready alternative. In the absence of any alternative, there is no recourse but to try to perfect what is at hand.

What was consistently expressed in the seminar, though, was a longing for a greater sense of community, of inclusiveness, of *égalité* and *fraternité*. The promises of democracy and capitalism—of liberalism—are unfilled in Latin America. There are too many economic (and so social) cleavages, too many left outside, wallowing in poverty, for a model of social organization grounded in the rights of the individual to satisfy. And the abject failures of communal political projects throughout the twentieth century do not justify the shortcomings of liberalism in Latin America. An impoverished peasant in the northeast of Brazil does not console himself by reflecting on the disasters of the collectivization of agriculture in Cambodia; a poor unemployed woman in Mexico City does not pause to think of the shortcomings of state enterprises in Poland.

There is an unease in Latin America with the inability to offer a more just, a more dignified, and more inclusive home for all Latin Americans. True, many are indifferent, frequently there are more immediate concerns, and a sense of fatalism is pervasive. But as happened at the seminar held at INCAE, when thoughtful Latin Americans stop to reflect on present conditions and trends, invariably there is discontent and worry over the inadequacy—or misfit—of liberalism to the needs of Latin America. Indeed, for some the region is all but bereft of a political beacon. For example, in an interview titled "Markets and States in Latin America," published in the fall–winter 2000–2001 issue of *PLAS Boletín*, one of Latin America's most distinguished economists, Pedro-Pablo Kuczynski, said:

> I'm very concerned about the lack of a vision on where Latin America is going. Where do we want to go, what's the scheme here? We seem to import ideas . . . but I'd like to see more ideas of our own as to where we are going to be in ten or fifteen years.

The absence of a vision is notable, and it retards discussion of social problems and their possible solution.

The thoughtful and articulate participants at the INCAE seminar did elaborate a host of ways in which Latin America could better meet the needs of its peoples. These suggestions could be accommodated within the prevailing framework of liberal democratic regimes and "free markets." There are certainly possibilities of calibrating democracies by changing the "rules of the game" and so providing different incentives to political actors. The same possibilities exist with the management of the economy. These reforms entail political battles, but it is politics with a lowercase p: struggles are local and issue-specific.

However, the call by young Latin Americans for a "new political culture" is truly ambitious. How can this task possibly be accomplished? Can it be achieved without some overarching analytical framework—an ideology—to provide coherence and intellectual guidance to the project? Can a new political culture, one sufficiently diffused that it remakes political and economic institutions, be forthcoming without strong leadership?

The desire for change in Latin America may be widespread. At least among well-educated and socially engaged young Latin Americans, there appears to be a remarkable consensus on what kinds of changes are needed. But although similar words and phrases keep cropping up— equality of opportunity, transparency, accountability, and so forth— there is no intellectual framework that embraces and orders systematically these disparate wishes. The absence of such a framework slows movement for reform and inevitably reduces efforts at reform to only piecemeal moves.

There is likewise no visible leadership for the revamping of state and society in Latin America. Who could lead the charge? Political parties, the natural candidates, appear limp, plagued by problems of management and of declining legitimacy in the eyes of the public. Much is made of "new social movements," but they are commonly preoccupied with a single issue (such as gender, ethnicity, or the environment) and, furthermore, are often elliptic—and even evanescent—in their political presence and import. Evangelical churches have mushroomed in Latin America, but they have eschewed a political agenda. The Catholic Church, under the leadership of Pope John Paul II, has addressed some political issues, but only in the most circumspect fashion. Universities are quiet. Those in business—the "private sector"—are atomized and, in any case, busy making money. There simply is no visible leadership for sustained and coherent political and economic change in Latin America.

Latin America begins the twenty-first century with an uneasy calm. There is political peace. Political passion—with vocal concern for the public good—is out of fashion, appearing to be futile. However, there are abundant and trenchant problems in the region. Much cloth remains to be cut.

# Illustrations

1. Lasar Segall, *Irrende Frauen* (Wandering Women). Woodcut, 1922. 23.9 by 28.9 cm. Private collection, New York. Photography, Bruce Schwarz.

2. Jean Charlot, untitled. Pencil on paper, 1925. 20.3 by 21.6 cm. Throckmorton Fine Art, New York. Photography, Bruce Schwarz.

3. Tina Modotti, *Mella's Typewriter* or *La técnica* (Mella's Typewriter or The Technique). Photograph, gelatin silver print, 1928. 22.9 by 19.1 cm. Throckmorton Fine Art, New York. Photography, Bruce Schwarz.

4. Leopoldo Méndez, untitled. Linoleum cut, ca. 1930s. 7.2 by 9.5 cm. Private collection, New York. Photography, Joseph Coscia.

5. Joaquín Torres-García, *Formas constructivas* (Constructive Forms). Pencil on paper, ca. 1930s. 21 by 14 cm. Throckmorton Fine Art, New York. Photography, Bruce Schwarz.

6. Diego Rivera, *Mineros del oro registrados al salir de la mina* (Gold Miners Being Searched As They Leave the Mine). Watercolor on paper, 1938. 29.2 by 30.5 cm. Throckmorton Fine Art, New York. Photography, Joseph Coscia.

7. Miguel Covarrubias, untitled. Lithograph, ca. 1940s. 31.8 by 24.1 cm. Throckmorton Fine Art, New York. Photography, Bruce Schwarz.

8. Héctor García, *Niño en el vientre de concreto* (Boy in Concrete Womb). Photograph, gelatin silver print, 1952. 35.6 by 27.9 cm. Throckmorton Fine Art, New York.

9. Francisco Morra, *Acaparadores y el pueblo* (Profiteers and the People). Linoleum cut, 1943. 15.9 by 15.2 cm. Private collection, New York. Photography, Joseph Coscia.

10. Wilfredo Lam, *Dialogue des mes lampes* (Dialogue of My Lamps). Etching, ca. 1975. 15.5 by 9.5 cm. Throckmorton Fine Art, New York. Photography, Bruce Schwarz.

11. Roberto Matta, untitled. Lithograph, ca. 1960s. 49.5 by 64.8 cm. Throckmorton Fine Art, New York. Photography, Joseph Coscia.

12. Flor Garduño, *Agua—Valle Nacional, Oaxaca, México* (Water—Valle Nacional, Oaxaca, Mexico). Photograph, gelatin silver print, 1982. 30.5 by 22.9 cm. Throckmorton Fine Art, New York.

13. Nahum Zenil, *Crímenes sociólogicos series IV* (Sociological Crimes Series IV). Woodcut with aquatint, 1988. 20.3 by 12.1 cm. Throckmorton Fine Art, New York. Photography, Bruce Schwarz.

14. Luis González Palma, *El soldado* (The Soldier). Photograph, gelatin silver print with bitumen, 1993. 50.8 by 50.8 cm. Throckmorton Fine Art, New York. Photography, Bruce Schwarz.

15. Marta Pérez Bravo, *Para ayudar a un hermano 2/3* (To Help a Brother 2/3). Photograph, gelatin silver print, 1994. 100 by 80 cm. Throckmorton Fine Art, New York.

16. Alexander Apóstol, *Crucigrama 2/7* (Crossword Puzzle 2/7). Photograph, toned gelatin silver print with graphite, 1995. 49.5 by 36.8 cm. Throckmorton Fine Art, New York.

17. José Bedia, *Invocación* (Invocation). Acrylic on canvas, 1997. 40.6 by 30.5 cm. Throckmorton Fine Art, New York. Photography, Bruce Schwarz.

# A Note about Sources

As a graduate student at Cornell University, I worked with a coterie of colleagues who frequently referred to "fugitive documents." The informal term, as I came to understand, is used for a gamut of material that is rich with information—and so of use to scholars—but is not "published." Examples include mimeographed reports from government ministries, evaluations of projects by nongovernmental organizations, irregularly published newsletters, printed copies of speeches, pamphlets, and the like. In poor countries, such as those of sub-Sahara Africa, these sources of information predominate. Few books and journals are published. Newspapers and magazines exist, but coverage of issues is often incomplete. "Fugitive documents" frequently provide more depth, even though their format and style vary, hindering comparisons.

The World Bank and the International Monetary Fund describe nearly all the nation-states of Latin America as "middle-income countries." Despite higher per capita incomes, though, even such countries as Mexico, with a population of 100 million, have books published with printings of only one thousand to three thousand copies. And while some publishing firms are well established, others have a precarious existence and a poor distribution of their books. What you see in one bookstore you may never again see elsewhere. Academic journals in the region exist, but they tend to publish less empirically grounded analysis than is common elsewhere. So in Latin America, too, information about social, political, and economic trends is often best found in "fugitive documents." And even books, with their imprint, often end up being "fugitives."

The emergence of electronic databases and the Internet also accentuate an emphasis on divergent sources that, while they augment other sources of information, share the possible shortcomings of all "fugitive documents." These potential weaknesses are serious. "Fugitive documents" are, at least possibly: (1) ephemeral, (2) not conducive to comparative analysis, (3) difficult for others to locate and so consult, and—

most serious—(4) fraught with problems of reliability and validity. Statistics are always suspect. But when they are published in a "fugitive document (or website)" it is more difficult to gauge—or guess—their reliability and validity.

The intent here to portray Latin America in an immediate way has led to a reliance on personal testimony, observation, and, above all, on an eclectic array of "fugitive documents." The methodological limitations and risks assumed are considerable. Individuals whose personal histories are recounted here all have public lives, and so there is at least a check on the most gross forms of embellishment. The reliability of what is retold from "fugitive documents" is surely problematic at times, but every effort has been made to check at least the parameters of bold facts and statistics presented by the use of multiple (and independent) sources. Still, statistics presented should be seen as offering more a sense of a tendency or trend rather than some precise (and accurate) reckoning. The validity of any particular configuration of facts and figures—or the extent to which one can generalize from individual experiences—is always open to interpretation, with reasonable individuals reaching different conclusions. I have made a good-faith effort to be sensible.

Footnotes have been avoided in the text, in large part because most sources of information are anything but "readily available." A bibliography follows of the principal sources employed. The bibliography includes studies referred to in the text.

# Bibliography

Ades, Dawn. *Art in Latin America: The Modern Era, 1820–1980*. New Haven: Yale University Press, 1989.

Alcelay, Carlos. "Tal como somos." *Cambio 16* (January 31, 1994): 10–15.

Alponte, Juan María. "La ciudad de México: Ninguna solución al margen del proyecto de nación." *Rino 29* (winter 1998): 4–7.

Aristide, Jean-Bertrand. *Eyes of the Heart*. Monroe, Maine: Common Courage Press, 2000.

Armstrong, Elizabeth, and Victor Zamudio-Taylor, with contributions by Miki Garcia, Serge Gruzinski, and Pablo Herkenhoff. *Ultra-Baroque: Aspects of Post–Latin American Art*. La Jolla, Calif.: Museum of Contemporary Art, San Diego, 2000.

Auerbach, Ruth. "Apóstol: Entre pasatiempos y Narciso." In *Pasatiempos: Alexander Apóstol*. Caracas: Sala Mendoza, 1998.

Bendesky, León. *México: De la eufora al sacrificio*. Mexico City: Edere, 1998.

Berger, Peter. "Four Faces of Global Culture." *The National Interest* (fall 1997): 23–29.

Bobbio, Norberto. *Liberalism and Democracy*. London: Verso, 1990. First published in Italy as *Liberalismo e democrazia* by Franco Angeli Libri.

Bourdieu, Pierre. *Acts of Resistance: Against the Tyranny of the Market*. New York: New Press, 1998. First published in France as *Contre-feux* by Editions Liber-Raisons d'Agir.

Brunetti, Aymo, Gregory Kisunko, and Beatrice Weder. "Institutional Obstacles for Doing Business: Data Description and Methodology of a Worldwide Private Sector Survey." Washington, D.C., 1998. Mimeographed.

Castañeda, Jorge. *Utopia Unarmed*. New York: Knopf, 1993.

Delgado, Richard, and Jean Stefancic. Introduction to *The Latino/a Condition: A Critical Reader*, pp. xvii–xix. Edited by Richard Delgado and Jean Stefancic. New York: New York University Press, 1998.

Domínguez, Jorge. "Free Politics and Free Markets in Latin America." *Journal of Democracy* 9 (October 1998): 70–84.

Elsom, Derek. *Smog Alert: Managing Urban Air Quality*. London: Earthscan, 1996.

*Encyclopedia of Latin American History and Culture*. New York: Charles Scribner's Sons, 1996.

"Ernesto Neto." Interview by Bill Arning in *Bomb* (winter 2000): 78–84.

Foglio, Omar. "Lo que el disco y la represión se llevaron: Prácticas sociales y mediaciones rockeras en la Avenida Revolución." In *La Revolución también es una calle: Vida cotidiana y prácticas culturales en Tijuana*, pp. 65–73. Edited by Roberto Castillo, Alfonso García, and Ricardo Morales. Tijuana: 15 Ayuntamiento and Universidad Iberoamericana Noroeste, 1996.

Fox, Vicente. "Mensaje al Congreso de la Unión." *Voz y Voto* 94 (December 15, 2000): 38–46.

Fukuyama, Francis. "The End of History?" *The National Interest* (summer 1989): 3–18.

Fundación Nacional para el Desarrollo (FUNDE). *Las hermanas y hermanos lejanos: Ausentes pero presentes*. San Salvador: FUNDE, 1997.

Fundación Natura. *La Reserva Ecológica Manglares-Churute*. Quito: Fundación Natura, 1992.

Guillermoprieto, Alma. "The Harsh Angel." *The New Yorker* (October 6, 1997): 104–111.

Hove, Chenjerai. *Shebeen Tales: Messages from Harare*. London: Serif, 1994. First published in the Netherlands as *Berichten uit Harare* by In de Knipscheer.

Hurtado, Osvaldo. *Gobernabilidad, democracia y pobreza*. Quito: Programa de las Naciones Unidas para el Desarrollo (PNUD), 1997.

Instituto Nacional de Estadística y Censos (Ecuador). "Contaminación industrial en Guayaquil." Guayaquil, n.d. Mimeographed.

Inter-American Development Bank. *Development beyond Economics: Economic and Social Progress in Latin America, 2000 Report*. Washington, D.C.: Inter-American Development Bank, 2000.

———. *Facing up to Inequality in Latin America: Economic and Social Progress in Latin America, 1998–1999 Report*. Washington, D.C.: Inter-American Development Bank, 1998.

International Institute for Management Development. *The World Competitiveness Yearbook 2000*. Lausanne: International Institute for Management Development, 2000.

Jacobs, Jerry. *The Mall: An Attempted Escape from Everyday Life*. Prospect Heights, Ill.: Waveland Press, 1994.

Kelly, Brian, and Mark London. *Amazon*. San Diego: Harcourt Brace Jovanovich, 1983.

Khilnani, Sunil. *The Idea of India*. New York: Farrar, Straus and Giroux, 1997.

Latinobarómetro. "*Cruces totales Latinobarómetro 1998*." Santiago, 1999. Mimeographed.

Laurance, William, Mark Cochrane, Scott Bergen, Philip Fearnside, Patricia Delamônica, Christopher Barber, Sammya D'Angelo, and Tito Fernandes. "The Future of the Brazilian Amazon." *Science* 291 (January 19, 2001): 438–439.

Lefkowitz, David. "Shopping and the Meaning of Life." *New Art Examiner* (April 1998): 30–33.

Lightner, Donald, and George Ware. "Workshop on Taura Syndrome of Penaeid Shrimp." Tucson, 1994. Mimeographed.

Lipton, Michael. *Why Poor People Stay Poor: Urban Bias in World Development*. Cambridge: Harvard University Press, 1977.

Lucie-Smith, Edward. *Latin American Art of the Twentieth Century*. London: Thames and Hudson, 1993.

Mainwaring, Scott. "The Surprising Resilence of Elected Governments." *Journal of Democracy* 10 (July 1999): 101–114.

Mainwaring, Scott, and Timothy Scully. "Introduction: Party Systems in Latin America." In *Building Democratic Institutions: Party Systems in Latin America*, pp. 1–34. Edited by Scott Mainwaring and Timothy Scully. Stanford: Stanford University Press, 1995.

Mark, Joan. *The Silver Gringo: William Spratling and Taxco*. Albuquerque: University of New Mexico Press, 2000.

"Markets and States in Latin America: An Interview with Pedro-Pablo Kuczynski." Interview by David Romo in *PLAS Boletín* (fall–winter 2000–2001): 2, 12–13.

Mato, Daniel. "Problems in the Making of Representations of All-Encompasing U.S. Latina/o–Latin American Transnational Identities." *The Latino Review of Books* 3 (spring/fall 1997): 2–7.

Mujeres 94. *Plataforma de las mujeres salvadoreñas, 1997–2000*. San Salvador: Mujeres 94, 1997.

Museu de Arte de São Paulo and Museu de Arte Moderna do Rio de Janeiro. *Marcia Grostein: Forma selvagem, 20 anos de percurso*. São Paulo and Rio de Janeiro: Museu de Arte de São Paulo and Museu de Arte Moderna do Rio de Janeiro, 1994.

Parra, Gustavo. *La conservación del Lago de Maracaibo: Diagnóstico ecológico y plan maestro*. Caracas: Lagoven, 1986.

Paz, Octavio. *Posdata*. Mexico City: Siglo XXI, 1979.

Plattner, Marc. "From Liberalism to Liberal Democracy." *Journal of Democracy* 10 (July 1999): 121–134.

Ramírez, Sergio. "Un país que se desangra." *El Semanario* (August 5–11, 1999): 6.

Reyes, Freddy. "Occidente: En sintonía con la dimensión ambiental." *Nosotros* (May/June 1994): 22–25.

Roberts, Kenneth. "Neoliberalism and the Transformation of Populism in Latin America: The Peruvian Case." *World Politics* 48 (October 1995): 82–116.

Sagástegui, Mildrette, and Alberto Valdez. *El distrito está muy federal*. Mexico City: Siglo XXXI, 1996.

Sanguinetti, Julio María. *Meditaciones del milenio: Los viejos y nuevos caminos de la libertad*. Montevideo: Arca, 1994.

Sarlo, Beatriz. *Escenas de la vida posmoderna: Intelectuales, arte y videocultura en la Argentina*. Buenos Aires: Ariel, 1994.

Scott, James. *Weapons of the Weak: Everyday Forms of Peasant Resistance*. New Haven: Yale University Press, 1985.

Seitz, William. *The Art of Assemblage*. New York: The Museum of Modern Art, 1961.

Spratling, William. *File on Spratling: An Autobiography*. Boston: Little, Brown and Company, 1967.

Stam, Robert. *Tropical Multiculturalism: A Comparative History of Race in Brazilian Cinema and Culture*. Durham: Duke University Press, 1997.

Sullivan, Edward. *Aspects of Contemporary Mexican Painting*. New York: Americas Society, 1990.

Torres-García, Joaquín. "The Southern School." In Dawn Ades, *Art in Latin America: The Modern Era, 1820–1980*, pp. 320–322 (part of the app.). New Haven: Yale University Press, 1989.

United States Environmental Protection Agency (EPA). "Report of Recommendations to the Government of Ecuador Concerning the 'Taura Syndrome.'" Washington, D.C., 1994. Mimeographed.

Vargas Llosa, Mario. "América Latina y la opción liberal." In *El desafío neoliberal*, pp. 17–35. Edited by Barry Levine. Bogota: Editorial Norma, 1992.

Villoro, Juan. "Ciudad de México: Elogio de la mujer barbuda." *Equis* 9 (January 1999): 5–8.

Wiener, Raúl. *Fujimori: El elegido del pueblo: Balance del proceso político en el Perú*. Lima: Graphos 100 Editores, 1996.